You Moved My Life

About the Book

All of us have been students at some stage, a stage that is the threshold of a new future. During this time, it is teachers who shape our minds and mould our characters. As Henry Adams has said, "A teacher affects eternity."

You Moved My Life: Heartwarming stories of Teachers who mentored and taught us to dream is a collection of thirty-nine touching stories and essays about favourite teachers who left an indelible imprint on the minds and hearts of their students. Famous CEOs, Vice-chancellors, scientists, doctors, industry doyens, civil servants, writers and educators have written these narratives to pay tributes to their favourite teachers in India and America. The endearingly written stories recreate the picture of the model teacher in the school, college or university classroom working with dedication and devotion. The running theme is the same: Our Teachers changed our lives.

You Moved My Life is a perfect gift to give to your teacher, a prize book for students, an inspirational book to give to aspiring and new teachers. It is a great possession for anyone who has ever been involved in education.

YOU MOVED MY LIFE

Heartwarming stories of Teachers who mentored and taught us to dream

Edited by
Prof Dr (Ms) Viney Kirpal

NEW DAWN PRESS, INC.
USA • UK • INDIA

New Dawn Press Group

Published by New Dawn Press Group
New Dawn Press, Inc., 244 South Randall Rd # 90, Elgin, IL 60123
e-mail: sales@newdawnpress.com

New Dawn Press, 2 Tintern Close, Slough, Berkshire, SL1-2TB, UK
e-mail : ndpuk@mail.newdawnpress.com

New Dawn Press (An Imprint of Sterling Publishers (P) Ltd.)
A-59, Okhla Industrial Area, Phase-II, New Delhi-110020
e-mail : info@sterlingpublishers.com
www.sterlingpublishers.com

*You Moved My Life : Heartwarming stories of
Teachers who mentored and taught us to dream*
Copyright © 2004 by Viney Kirpal
ISBN 1 932705 41 4

All rights are reserved. No part of this publication may be reproduced, stored in a retrieval system or transmitted, in any form or by any means, mechanical, photocopying, recording or otherwise, without prior written permission of the original publisher.

PRINTED IN INDIA

To My Teachers

Miss Maggie, KG
Convent of Jesus and Mary, New Delhi

Mrs Rosario, Std II
Convent of Jesus and Mary, Ambala

Mrs Puesch, Std VII
St Mary's Academy, Meerut

Dr (Miss) K D Shroff
Nowrosjee Wadia College, Pune

Professor S Nagarajan
University of Poona, Pune

all the **Teachers** of the **World**
whose dedication this book celebrates

A woman attended her 20-year high school reunion. There she encountered her freshman year art teacher. She told him that she decided to go to college as a result of his inspiration, and that she was an art professor, now, at a large state university.

At the end of the evening's festivities, the teacher searched out his former student, shook her hand and said, "Thank you for saying those nice things about my teaching. You've really made my day." "You're welcome," said the woman as she hugged him. "But let me thank you – you've made my life!"

— *Author unknown*

Foreword

Writing the foreword for this fantastic collection of reminiscences is no easy job. The autobiographical flavour of the contributions is so engaging that one wishes to ask the writers to tell more about themselves as young learners and also fill out the sketches of their teachers with some more telling strokes. At the same time, one gets lost in one's own past and reminiscences come back hauntingly.

Their recollections, seen against the background of their reflective and mature adulthood, instill life into the stock educational words 'teaching' and 'learning'. They also make readers like me peep into the past and recall school and college experiences of which a variety of teachers formed part. In my recollection, there are a few teachers who could be inspirers and affectionate guides. But there are the indifferent ones too. Also, some are even harsh and hard. All this needs to be critically analysed by expert psychologists.

This collection of tributes to teachers reminds me of what the ancient Tamil poet Tiru Valluvar has said so appropriately: "The peculiar character of learning is that it is a double source of pleasure, an intrinsic joy to him who has the knowledge, and a source of happiness to others that benefit by it." The positive side of the picture delineated in these reminiscences is certainly important for teacher-education programme as case-study material. From this standpoint the publication is an extremely valuable addition to educational literature. I congratulate Dr Viney Kirpal on her noteworthy contribution.

29 January 2004
Chitra Naik
Chairperson
Indian Institute of Education, Pune

Acknowledgements

I was helped by many while compiling this book. I gratefully acknowledge their contributions :
1. All my contributors to whom their teachers have meant so much and who have written this collaborative book.
2. S K Ghai, chief Managing Director, Sterling Publishers Pvt Ltd, New Delhi and his enthusiastic team.
3. K S Venkatachalam's "Principal Lesson" reprinted with permission from *The Times of India*, Mumbai (14 July, 2003).
4. R K Laxman's extract from his *The Tunnel of Time: An Autobiography* (first published in Viking by Penguin Books India, (P), 1998. Copyright R K Laxman. Taken from internet from the link, "Teacher as Transformer." http://www.ncte-in.org/contrib/laxman.htm. Reprinted with author's permission.
5. Geetanjali Patole, Sub-editor, *Pune Times of India*, Pune.
6. G K K Singh, Trustee, GREAT Foundation, Pune.
7. Devi Daswani, Administrative Officer, GREAT Foundation, Pune.
8. Yasin A Shaikh, Administrative Associate, GREAT Foundation, Pune.
9. Kanika Thakur, Assistant, GREAT Foundation, Pune.
10. Archana Shinde, Pune

30 January 2004

Viney Kirpal
GREAT Foundation, Pune

Contents

Foreword by Chitra Naik	vii
Acknowledgements	ix
Introduction	xv

Part I
School Teachers

1.	Power of Choice – *Lila Poonawalla*	3
2.	Father for All Seasons – *Gen N S Cheema*	6
3.	The Eklavya Era – *Sharu Rangnekar*	9
4.	12 O'Clock – *R K Saboo*	12
5.	Perfect Leaf – *R K Laxman*	17
6.	Voice Wisdom – *Partap Sharma*	19
7.	Principal Lesson – *K S Venkatachalam*	32
8.	The Write Angle – *Cyprian D'Souza*	34
9.	A Lesson Learnt by Heart – *Ratna Khemani*	37
10.	Turning Point – *Padmaja P Godbole*	40
11.	Indebted for a Lifetime – *P S Palande*	43
12.	Sister Superior: Above Par – *Gayatri Chatterjee*	47
13.	The Art of Conquering Numbers – *Nalini Swamidasan*	51
14.	When Teachers Become Friends – *Nandita Saikia*	54
15.	To Sir, with Love – *S K Savanur*	57
16.	Irreverently, Ever Yours – *Anjali Ray*	59

17.	A Habit of Benevolence – *Geeta Sundar*	63
18.	No "Short Corners" – *Arnavaz Damania*	66
19.	Passing the Torch On – *Ashok Kelkar*	68

PART II
COLLEGE AND UNIVERSITY TEACHERS

20.	A Prayer for Talib – *Amrik Singh*	77
21.	Electricity at First Sight – *V V Athani*	81
22.	A Future in the Past – *Sushma Varma*	83
23.	A Scroll of Honour – *P C Shejwalkar*	86
24.	The Mathematical Comic – *Roop Karnani*	89
25.	A Legacy Unforgotten – *Rehana Ghadially*	93
26.	The Physics of Humanity – *Subroto Roy*	96
27.	Nobel Teacher – *A N Maheshwari*	98
28.	Great and Godly – *Kumarendra Mallick*	104
29.	Lady Pacific – *Devika Bose*	110
30.	That Touch of Brightness – *Kudlu Chithprabha*	114
31.	Literary Blessing – *Shridhar B Gokhale*	118
32.	Potter among Pupils – *Viney Kirpal*	122
33.	Some Reminiscences of My Teachers – *S Nagarajan*	129
34.	Investment of a Lifetime – *Sampat Singh*	143
35.	Net Gain – *A A Mutalik-Desai*	147
36.	When Saints Walk the Earth – *P G Joshi*	152
37.	Coffee with Archie – *Ingrid Arnesen*	156
38.	The Excavation of a True Mind – *Sugandha Johar*	159
39.	Perfect Music – *Gayatri Moorthy*	162

About the Contributors   165

Introduction

We are what we are because of our teachers. This is the recurring theme of this book about favourite teachers. Former students have taken a backward glance at their life in school, college or university to write about those teachers who have contributed to their lives in a profound way. Some have extolled their schoolteachers while others have written about their college or university teachers. A few have commemorated both. Some stories tell of more than one teacher, while others recall the one teacher who had influenced them most. Some describe their Indian and foreign teachers in India, and others, their Indian and foreign teachers in American universities. The gallery of dedicated teachers is truly awesome. Great teachers stride through the pages leaving indelible imprints of their colossal personalities and stature. The fifty odd men and women, whom their students recall with admiration, are truly unforgettable.

No wonder their students step back in time to record their gratitude to them. They recreate the personalities of their special teachers the way they had come across to them when they were their pupils. Each documents the special meaning that his or her teacher had endowed upon their lives and recalls the genesis of their relationship that had originated at a time when they were callow, vulnerable, confused, and beset by self-doubt.

As they record their teachers' kindness, thoughtfulness, creativity, and knowledge, famous CEOs like Cyprian D'Souza, former Vice-Chancellors like Professors Amrik Singh and

A N Maheshwari, civil servants like P S Palande, army generals like Gen N S Cheema, industry doyens like Lila Poonawalla, and Raja Saboo (also India's past Rotary International President), writers like Partap Sharma, scientists like Bhatnagar awardee Kumarendra Mallick, Magsaysay awardee and cartoonist R K Laxman, and many others pen the biographies of their teachers with great warmth, and in an endearing manner. The warmth they exude is the warmth that they had felt for their teachers when they were young children or mere youths. Though the ages of the writers vary from twenty to eighty – the glow of warmth remains unchanged over time.

As one reads the stories of these remarkable teachers, one is struck by one persistent thought, "Were these teachers or were they great leaders?" Did these teachers know what role they were playing in the lives of their students? Did they have a vision of their role? Did they plan in advance to give their students all that they gave them, or was it spontaneous? Did they consciously try to educate them in values, character and attitude? Did they do this knowing how hard was the task they had taken up? Did they do it fully aware of what intractable material human beings are made of? Surely these teachers were not ordinary men and women. Not content to look upon teaching as a job, they had gone beyond the call of their profession to play the important role only a leader can play.

The teachers who live in the pages of this book first made their impact in the classroom. They taught creatively, and took pains to spice their classes with anecdotes and stories. They generated love for the subject by making their teaching as stimulating as possible. They were innovative; they worked hard and they made their students work hard. The students obeyed because their teachers were knowledgeable and they cared. These teachers could skate through the world of knowledge and bring depth as well as breadth to their teaching. They could inspire their students intellectually and move them emotionally. They also knew how to ignite the quest for learning, sometimes through outdoor classes, or a visit to a movie, or through a hobby. They definitely broke through classroom walls.

The model teachers are also remembered for the encouragement they had given their students. Former students recall their teachers' kind and inspiring words, their fairness in rewarding them with good marks for good work, and counsel when they erred. They laud them for their faith in them, for recognizing their potential, long before they themselves had done so. Their teachers had challenged them to perform beyond their capacity by planting dreams in their heads, and urging them forward when they themselves weren't aware of their own capabilities. Each contributor has recorded a similar story of debt to their teacher.

What really fascinates one is the way these teachers knew just how difficult it is to be a student. The difficulty of not understanding a language, the inability to grasp abstract mathematical concepts, the difficulty of not being able to relate to urban culture, the difficulty of just being young and unable to understand many things about oneself, one's relationships, one's friends, one's environment. The special teacher is remembered with special regard for that one quality – namely the *ability to support* a student when he or she needed it the most, and in the best possible manner.

Whether it is the nun who was worried that two of her pupils had not eaten, or the teacher who cycled daily to a Std X student's home to coach him in sports and save him time for studies, or the teacher who tried to make up to his students for their having missed their holiday to attend an extra class, or the teacher who weaned away a student from the habit of taking tranquilizers – all these are extraordinary acts of empathy, concern and understanding on the part of teachers.

This is also the quality of great leaders. An army general can inspire his soldiers to lay down their lives because of the solid support he gives them. A great CEO can inspire ordinary employees to give extraordinary performances. These teachers, whether in the primary, secondary or tertiary levels, were of the mettle of great generals and CEOs. They got the best out of their students because they walked beside them.

It is this quality that each narrator in the book has recalled with the nostalgia of admiration, joy and affection. Each story has a different style which gives a distinct beauty to the narration. Sometimes one hears the rhythms of a vernacular language, and sometimes of an English convent school. What binds the storytellers – all achievers and eminent professionals – is their act of having stepped out of their present status to respectfully pay glowing, well-deserved tributes to their dedicated, selfless and humble teachers. The unconditional gratitude to their teachers who had given them so much, without asking for anything in return, is the highest offering – *the real guru dakshina* – that any student can ever give to a teacher.

This book truly inspires all teachers to *earn* a similar offering from their students. Yes, *earn* it, because out of the hundred odd teachers who teach, there is perhaps just one per cent chance of getting selected by one's student for that unique honour that has been bestowed on these teachers, and even that one per cent chance can bypass a teacher if the student has more than one favourite teacher!

Hidden in the stories are the secrets of becoming a great teacher — learned, inspiring, devoted, creative, courageous and compassionate. Concealed in them are the numerous techniques and pedagogical methods that creative teachers use. The book holds a wealth of learning for every teacher.

Indeed, every person who reads this book will feel influenced and inspired to excel in the profession he or she belongs to.

Introduction

Students especially will draw inspiration both from the lives of the teachers and the writers who have narrated the stories. While the lives of the teachers exemplify the best qualities of outstanding teachers, the writers too were of the stuff just waiting to fulfill their teacher's aspirations. When teachers inspired, they (the students) worked hard, and willingly walked that extra mile to realise their teachers' and their own dreams. Every young student who reads the book will see what it takes to reach the top. It is not what you are born with that takes you there but what you become by developing your knowledge, your skills and attitude. You could be born in a poor home or you could begin schooling in a village but you could end up as a CEO or an eminent scientist. The teachers were the catalysts; the students their eager disciples, happy to let the former turn their lives around. The relationship is mutual.

Thus, every person will benefit enormously from reading these inspiring stories. You can read one story at a time or you can read them in one sitting. The teachers we meet in these pages are *role models* for every teacher who ever wanted to excel. Their vision, their ability to work against all odds with dedication and devotion, and lead their mentees from the front has been felt all along. This book is a commemoration to the spirit of these great teachers by the grateful students. We are now sure our favourite teachers will live in everyseheart (as they live in ours), and continue to show the way to thousand others.

Viney Kirpal

Part I

School Teachers

I am your student.
Care for me, Teach me,
Help me to be a good person,
I will remember you forever.

– *Pat Krushen*

Power of Choice
Lila Poonawalla

Success for a teacher means motivating students to believe that they are smart – not stupid – and helping students develop self-images that will lift them to heights they had never dreamed of before. My teacher, Ms Manek Sunderji, did just that. She made a tremendous impact on my life. I was not a very bright student. In fact until Standard VIII, I always used to be promoted, never passed. It was she who changed my life.

She made me believe that each one of us has a huge reservoir of untapped potential for achievement, success, happiness, health and greater prosperity. It's like a huge unexplored ocean or a new continent, a world of possibilities waiting to be released and channeled toward some great good. She made me realise that every step along the way to achieving a goal is just as important as the last step. It is not the achievement of a goal that is so important; it is what you become in the process that is. Today, I am thankful to her for all the values that she taught me. Maybe she did not realise the influence she was having on me, but the impact that she made on me continues to sustain me till today.

I was very fond of playing baseball. I used to feel great when I hit the ball and reached the first base. I felt that I had done my job and thought that then it was up to the other players to hit so that I could move on till I reached the home base. She, through her unassuming ways, made me realise that making it to the first base gives you only a few points but it is with the support of the complete team that you are able to win and that just making it to the bases did not count. She made me turn a new leaf. Her lessons have had a far-reaching impact on my role as a corporate head.

Ms Sunderji also taught me to dream. She made me understand that people who can dream are the ones most likely to realise them. After all goals are targets based on your dreams that get transferred into a vision so as to succeed. These were the kind of inputs that made me set a dream for my team when I became the Managing Director of Alfa Laval. My slogan for the company was 'One Team One Goal' and we set ourselves a BRC – the Billion Rupee Challenge. The company then had a turnover of only Rupees 400 million. We wanted to more than treble it in three years. Yes, it was a 'dream'. But my teacher had taught me to dream and to set goals carefully and thoughtfully. Such goals give motivational direction. At first you turn your dreams into visions and then you convert your visions into goals. Once you can do that half the task is accomplished; it is only the implementation that remains. And in my case, the implementation also worked. We all know the success story of Alfa Laval.

My teacher also taught me a lot about discipline, which I cherish until today. Those who have interacted with me know how true this is. *Self-discipline, she taught me, is the ability to make yourself do what you should do when you should do it, whether you feel like it or not.* It is easy to do something when you feel like doing it. It's only when you don't feel like doing something and yet you force yourself to do it anyway, that you move your life and career around.

She taught me that any day we wish it, we can discipline ourselves to change. Any day we wish to we can start a new activity. Any day we wish to we can open the book that opens our mind to knowledge beyond boundaries. Any day we wish it, we can start the process of life change. We can do it immediately, or the next week, or the next month, or the next year. We can also do nothing. We can pretend rather than perform. And if the idea of having to change ourselves makes us uncomfortable, we can remain as we are. The choice is ours. She certainly helped me to learn all this and make the right choices.

Often she used to speak wise words to me. One day, she told me "Lila, you have the ability to transform every area of your life — and it all begins with your very own self-discipline. Remember it is the power of choice." On another occasion, she told me, "Nothing in life is to be feared. It is only to be understood."

As I conclude this tribute, I wish to dedicate a small poem to my teacher, my mentor, my guide. This poem summarises her teachings which transformed my life forever:

> Don't wish it were easier, wish you were better.
> Don't wish for fewer problems, wish for more skills.
> Don't wish for fewer challenges, wish for more wisdom.
> Let others lead small lives, but not you.
> Let others argue over small things, but not you.
> Let others cry over small hurts, but not you.
> Let others leave their future in someone else's hands,
> but not you.
> Remember, if you do what you decide,
> then the 'future belongs to you'.

Thank you my teacher for contributing to the changes in my life.

Father for All Seasons

N S Cheema

Late in 1938, three young priests arrived after studying in the UK at St Vincent's School, Pune, from Switzerland. Rev Father A Oesch, a handsome, firm, no-nonsense man, Rev Father R Schoch, a sharp, provocative and a 'go gather' man, who could get around just anybody and Rev Father Haefeli, a short, stocky and happy man who could do just anything with his hands. Though very close to each other the three were as diverse as human beings ever can be.

Rev Father Oesch got down to all activities that were so dear to him, teaching German, looking after the school museum and his friendly eight-foot python, and spending time on the sports field with young boys, especially those interested in athletics.

Rev Father Oesch himself had been an accomplished athlete, tennis player and mountaineer. St Vincent's and specially Pune owe him much for his contribution to athletics. He was a dedicated man who could and did sport talent and spared no effort to cultivate it for the best possible results. Unfortunately, resources and technology for sport were very limited in those early years and everything was managed through self-help and improvisation. Hard work and experience made up for the lack of exposure of a coaching institution. When the exams came near, to save the athlete some time for study, Rev Father Oesch would cycle to the student's house to coach him on site. With him, the relationship with his students in class and on the sports field was a solemn mission which knew no bars.

In the early days and through the forties all the three Fathers moved around on their German bicycles. They introduced in the school the culture of the occasional bicycle picnics on holidays and weekends to Koregaon, Sinhgad, Moshi and other places around Pune. Usually all the three – Schoch, Oesch and Haefeli – went together. These picnics inculcated tremendous spirit of esprit de corps and confidence amongst the students. This spirit in a way helped a lot to improve the performance in class and on the sports field.

Rev Father Oesch was basically a 'family man' who had endeared himself not only to his school's sportsmen and students, but also to the families of many young people; advising, blessing and helping them whenever they needed it. He was a man of spartan habits and tremendous discipline. He did suffer some setbacks in health, at least on three occasions. Once serious enough for him to be evacuated back to Switzerland. However, each time, it was superlative will and determination which saw him back to recovery and good health.

In the Fathers' house, he was possibly among the few who was in regular touch with his family members – mother, brother, sister-in-law, nephews and nieces. Here in Pune, Father did have a very warm relationship and love for our family, specially for my late father Dr G S Cheema. Father Oesch could relate with all of us. I do not remember any birthday when there was not a word of greetings for me from Rev Father Oesch no matter where I was posted.

A dedicated man – dedicated to his work, to his students and friends – a man with a mission till the very last, he was a man who will be remembered by students all over the world for his selfless giving and purposeful life and associations.

His interests in life were varied. He introduced his 'boys' to nature, stones, reptiles, foliage, good reading and so much more. His love for St Vincent's was legendary. When his second bout of severe health problems occurred, he was advised rest and sent back to Switzerland. However after recovery, he made it clear to all concerned that there was nothing more in Switzerland for him and that he had to go back to St Vincent's and his boys to whom he had dedicated his whole life, and of course, he did come back.

For nearly five centuries, the community of priests has lived an amazing story in the history of the world, serving humanity in new and unexpected ways. They are always on the move, ready to change countries, ready to improve and build people. They are expected to do anything, anywhere to teach students and build character. They are there to share their vision and create a permanent place in the hearts of their students. Their ultimate enquiry as teachers can be encapsulated in three questions:

What have I done for my students?
What am I doing for my students?
What will I do for my students?

The Eklavya Era

Sharu S Rangnekar

Technology has an impact on the role of the teacher. It affects the very selection of what is taught since the curriculum has also to fulfill the requirements of the student. In ancient times, a typical Brahmin went to his guru's ashram for about twelve years and had all the education he required, for the rest of his life. He normally had only one guru and the knowledge of that guru was adequate for his entire career.

Today, a typical student has to gather knowledge from over a hundred teachers from various educational institutions. In the last generation, the coaching classes have come up to supplement the input of the formal educational institutions. The role of the coaching classes has increased in importance and many students pay more money to the coaching classes than to the formal educational institutions. Furthermore, they are seen giving less and less time to the formal institutions as compared to the time that they give to the coaching classes. In many educational institutions – particularly at the college level – the attendance in formal classes is as low as 30 per cent while the coaching classes have over 90 per cent attendance. The reason is obvious. The students feel that the time and money spent on coaching classes give them better returns than the time and money spent on formal education.

The question is, what is the role of a teacher in the formal educational process?

The teacher in the coaching class normally gets the last ten years' examination papers solved by the student and this improves his or her ability to get better scores in their examination. The teacher in the formal educational institution has to 'cover' the curriculum and give the 'knowledge'. This may not improve the ability of the student to score well in the examination.

In the competitive world of today, the examination score has assumed great importance. The periodic leakage of examination papers is an indication as to what the students (and their parents) will do to improve their examination score.

If we look back at our own lives today and catalog the hundred odd teachers in the formal educational institutions who taught us, we can remember only four or five of them. The rest are forgotten.

Talking about myself, I vividly remember my first Sanskrit teacher. The very first period that he came, he told us, "Boys, you are lucky!" We wondered how we had suddenly become lucky. We asked, "Why?" "Do you know what you are going to study?" he asked. "Sanskrit," we said. He asked, "Do you know what Sanskrit is?" "A language", we said. One of us said, "A scoring subject." In those days students could score over 90 per cent marks only in three subjects: Mathematics, Science and Sanskrit. The teacher said, "You are all wrong. Sanskrit is not just a language or a scoring subject. It is the key to five thousand years of culture. With this one key the whole treasury is yours." We were 40 students. Not everybody believed him – but 10 or 12 of us understood just what he meant.

After my matriculation, Sanskrit was of no use to me either in my chemical engineering or my MBA. But I still read Sanskrit. The teacher did not only teach the language. What he did was

The Eklavya Era

to arouse curiosity about the language. *Once curiosity is aroused, the student keeps on learning by himself* using every opportunity to satisfy his desire for knowledge.

In short, he becomes an Eklavya.

'That is the real role of the teacher. To create Eklavyas!

In the age of the Internet, vast amounts of knowledge are available on the website. Learning is becoming easier, like drinking water from a hosepipe. A person interested in a subject can get any amount of knowledge from the website, without a teacher.

Thus, an era of Eklavyas has started. Those teachers who can arouse the interest of their students in any particular subject will create in them a thirst for knowledge, which they will try to satisfy in every way, including visits to the website.

That is what teachers are supposed to do. And that is what my teacher did.

12 O'clock

R K Saboo

It was 1946. I had finished my Class VIII in my native place in Rajasthan at the peak of World War II and the rest in a suburban school with a vernacular medium. My father, on getting promoted, moved to the corporate headquarters in Kolkata and I too was naturally required to move to a school in the metro. I suppose admission in school at that time was not a big problem as they are now but to get into a reputed convent was beyond my comprehension. In fact, I vividly remember that I had no idea of what I was getting into when my father told me that I had to go for an interview to St Xavier's, the reputed English medium school of Kolkata, where the upper classes sent their children.

Till then I had seen only two schools – both in the remote areas of Rajasthan – and being ignorant of anything different, I entered the premises of St Xavier's on the appointed day with no element of fear or bravado. However, this confidence was short-lived and soon to be replaced by awe, on my encountering for the first time a totally new and unknown, alien ambience. I was nervous and even mortified when I was ushered alone into the room of a person with a long flowing gray beard, dressed in a white gown. He was very soft spoken but so much was I swollen by my own freight that when he asked me what my age was, I replied "12 O'clock" instead of saying "12 years". He laughed and I thought I had it. Maybe I also felt somewhat relieved that I would not be admitted to this school after that faux pas. But soon he put me at ease and joked with me. I was not able to comprehend him fully but this much I could understand that I had been admitted. Maybe he took this raw, uncouth lad as a challenge. That was Father Van Buynder, a Jesuit priest who was to be my mentor, significantly reshaping my life and putting me into a new mould.

Father Van Buynder was not only the class teacher for Class X, i.e. Matriculation but he was also the head of the matriculation section, which included both Classes IX and X. Admitted to Class IX, known as Prep-Matric then, I was probably the slowest in the class. As it is I was not among the brightest in my earlier school and now the cultural difference, the English medium, the urbanized classmates in the new school made me the most vulnerable victim of an inferiority complex. I was hardly able to keep pace with the class or with what was going on around me in the school.

In spite of that stifling atmosphere where everything appeared alien to me I felt that there was one person I could approach any time and without any fear. Father Van Buynder had given me that liberty and courage without explicitly saying so. Even though he was not my class teacher, I could confide in him my problems, my complexes, my anxieties. But one positive trait that I had – the will to make it – was, I think, detected by Father Van Buynder, for at every step he used to encourage me and infuse me with confidence. He helped me strengthen this attitude of 'not to quit' and found ways to make me lift up my spirits, to seek enthusiasm in new activities. He had a remarkable way of not telling what he wanted his students to learn and yet achieving the objective. Empathetically, painstakingly and firmly he worked with me on my English, be it grammar, conversation or pronunciation. He taught me the ways of the school culture, the discipline, about sociability amongst peers and how to overcome my inferiority complex.

Not only with me was he like that, but with practically every student under him and especially with those who were weak. To them he gave his special attention as if he were molding raw mud, first into clay and then into an artwork.

By the time I came to Class X, I had risen to the middle level of performance in class. I had also become reasonably immersed in the school ambience but somehow I felt that though I was accepted by the urbanized lot of my classmates, I had not quite become part of them.

Father Van Buynder had been talking to me about me and my family's background, my father's work place, to get to know me better. One day, he suggested that I should invite the whole class for a picnic to the Birla Jute Mills premises along the Hooghly River. This unit was looked after by my father and I would have no difficulty in organizing the picnic but would the other students come, would Father Van Buynder himself agree to participate, was my dilemma. He did not have to tell the class much because he put his name first on the list of acceptances. This picnic was great fun for everyone but more than that it was a turning point for me.

From then on, I became an integral part of the class. And this was the first of a series of picnics we had, each one with a different flavour, meticulously planned and guided by Father Van Buynder considering the circumstances of the host student always making him feel his picnic was the best.

In Class X, Father Van Buynder taught us all the subjects, except Hindi, Sanskrit and Mathematics. He used to organize elocution tests, debates, general knowledge quizzes and art exhibitions and tell me what I could do or help me infuse some creative elements, which otherwise were totally absent in me. I remember a particular class of Moral Science in which he asked each one of us how we could prove the presence of God. When my turn came, he came close to me and looking straight into my eyes, asked me to answer the question. Instantly, I slapped the student sitting next to me. My friend was about to react, so was Father Van Buynder but I immediately asked my friend, "Did it hurt you?" He replied, "Of course, it did." And I said, "You see, Father, he can feel the pain but he cannot see it. This is how we feel God even though we do not see Him." This put me on top of the class, my answer being adjudged the best.

I must make detailed mention of the "stamp collection" hobby he had initiated among each of his students. I remember distinctly that Father Van Buynder, himself a great stamp collector, encouraged every young student to take on this hobby. I too got on with this. Being originally from Belgium he probably had contacts all over the world and had a good stock of used stamps from different countries. He used to sell one match box full of assorted, used stamps for one anna, now equal to about 6 paise. This was no price but just a medium to sow the seeds of this hobby.

This was his way of bringing the world into the classroom and lodging it inside the minds of the young students. Through this hobby he created a special interest in geography, history, social sciences including nature, inventions and industrial activities, and other spheres pertaining to human development. Through this singular interest of stamps he developed diverse bonds with his students. However, to some of us stamp collection became a philatelic passion going beyond our school days.

I gave up my stamp collection soon after I got into business but one of us, a classmate who too started with me, Devki N Jatia rose to an international level in philately. He became one of the top stamp collectors of the world and ultimately was Chairman of the International Jury on Philately; a proud achievement for the school, for the class of 1948-49, for Father Van Buynder and for all Indian philatelists. We basked in the glory of Devki Jatia.

When I passed Matric I may not have been one of the top students in my class, but I certainly was an extrovert. I was not an eloquent speaker but I had a confident personality and I could stand firmly on my feet, hold my head high and keep my back straight.

I do not know if I have spelt Father Van Buynder's name correctly but I do know that the imprint he left within me will remain unerased till my last breath.

Perfect Leaf

R K Laxman

One day, instead of leaving the class in charge of the monitor before stepping out to have a couple of puffs, he (the teacher) set up a task: we were ordered to draw a leaf, any leaf.

This was something new and exciting and all the boys at once set about it enthusiastically. We were soon absorbed in the creative task. Some boys sat wondering trying to imagine a leaf. One fellow drew a banana leaf that was so big it went out of the wooden frame of the slate. Another boy, after pondering for a while and failing to visualize a leaf, announced loudly, "I am going to draw an elephant instead!" Thus we were so busily engaged that we had not even noticed the teacher either leaving or returning. A couple of loud thumps on the table with the cane brought us back to reality.

He asked us to queue up and began to critically examine our efforts one by one, murmuring comments and giving marks. Sometimes he twisted a boy's ear or brought the cane down on the leg of another. When it was my turn, he stared at the drawing for an alarmingly long time and asked me, "Did you draw it yourself Laxman?" I was frightened and stepped back, expecting a shower of blows. I replied, "You asked us to draw, sir . . . I sat there and drew..." fumbling for a safe excuse. But to my great surprise and joy he held my slate up before the class and announced, "Attention! Look how nicely Laxman has drawn the leaf!" He turned to me and said, "You will be an artist one day. Keep it up!" He gave me ten out of ten. He was very impressed by the perfect shape of my peepal leaf and the details of the veins branching out along the midrib. I had seen these leaves countless times strewn on the road under the peepal tree, and I could draw them effortlessly. I was inspired by this unexpected encouragement. *I began to think of myself as an artist in the making, never doubting that this was my destiny.*

Voice Wisdom

Partap Sharma

The first flash of realization that there was a whole alternative world of imagination locked away which would reveal itself to the thrill of appropriate sounds and words (*"Open sesame!"*) occurred, quite unexpectedly and almost accidentally, while I was still a student at a boarding school in the Himalaya mountains. This was not the first school I had attended. I had been in two other boardings, in another country, suffering loneliness and putting a brave face on it since the age of four.

Now, in my fourteenth year, it seemed there was no escaping the dullness of dormitories. My parents were always in distant, fascinating jungles, far from educational institutions, and I was reconciled to the fact that a highly-qualified Civil Engineer like my father was invariably going to be building dams in remote areas. It seemed I was banished forever, along with my younger brother, who too went into boarding when he turned four, to the dreariness of unfeeling institutions and the unremitting wrench of homesickness.

But, even within that parameter, Bishop Cotton School in Simla (now called Shimla) was unique. Not only did BCS stand at a higher altitude than any other public school in India but it positively looked down on any attitude that deviated from the traditions that accompanied the mortar board and gown. And these signs of academic ceremonial were worn by every member of the staff every day.

Indeed, a little farther down the hills was Lawrence School, Sanawar, a military institution of which Kipling had written so highly, exhorting the timid to "Send him to Sanawar and make a man of him, my son!" Well, BCS did not think of Sanawar as a rival – despite the boxing and sports matches held between them – but as a sister school because Sanawar, according to the undoubtedly-biased opinion of the boys of BCS, was full of 'sissies'. Doon School didn't even figure in the reckoning. It was way down in the foothills in another part of the Himalayan range.

So let me take you back to the rather tough days when Mr Fisher was headmaster and the staff flew about in their gowns, flapping frantically to keep pace with the lanky Freddie Brown, the acerbic Tubby Whitmarsh-Knight and the swiftly gliding Teddy Cuzzen. Everyone seemed somewhat athletic, very correct, rather British and certainly Oxbridge. The ragging, the fagging, the six cuts on the hand, the caning on the bottom, the copying down of the honour hoards, the Latin response of 'adsum' at roll-call – all echoed Rugby, Eton, Marlborough and other far-off screams of England. And no wonder, because the man who had come out to India after a teaching stint at Rugby and set up this school in the last century was none other than the man extolled as 'the perfect young Assistant Master' in the classic *Tom Brown's Schooldays*.

The Indian members of the staff were also rather high-powered. Mathematics was taught by the smiling, Buddha-like Mr Tuli whose ability with numbers was such that he could, while bouncing amiably on his feet, raise you to the power of infinity or reduce you to zero. Art was taught by a convoluted progressive from Calcutta who actually sold at exhibition. Hindi was taught by the writer Mohan Rakesh who subsequently achieved national fame as a playwright. And then suddenly, there was Mr Asrani the new English Literature master who, though he spoke well enough, had the appearance of a little hunched vulture that had just managed to stagger here after scavenging some garbage-dump in Lower Bazaar.

But, as it turned out, Mr Asrani proved to be one of the best teachers of all. His classes were always full of the unexpected and therefore kept us riveted. On his very first day, while we all sat dolefully fingering our copies of *Macbeth*, worrying what learned quiz he would devise to bore us further with the ponderousness of Shakespeare, he entered like the First Witch screeching and cackling, "When shall we three meet again? In thunder, lightning or in rain?"

It was an unforgettable entrance. But he wasn't content with that. Pointing to a boy at random, he gestured for a response. The boy quickly glanced at the text and replied, "When the hurly burly's done, when the battle's lost and won..."

As each new character entered the action, Mr Asrani pointed to another boy, and another, and another, till eventually the whole class was not just reading the words but performing the play in the collective imagination! The atmosphere became electric; we were all energized and fraught, full of eagerness but tense with anticipation – there was no telling where lightning might strike next. The one thing that was certain was that, most of all, Mr Asrani was enjoying himself. His delight made us follow him into realms of wonderment.

In due course, we discovered that Mr Asrani never talked of literature in the abstract, he displayed it like salesman presenting his wares. We were free to appreciate or criticize but first we had to show that we had the ability to buy what he was selling. In short, he wasn't going to waste his time with paupers of the spirit. We had to show that we were willing to pay with participation. If we were participants in the action then we had every right to say how it might be improved. Literature became a personal adventure.

Words sprang from the page and became drama. Years later, I looked up the origin of that word in the dictionary and found that, in Greek, it means 'a thing done'. Well, Mr Asrani demonstrated the power of art to us daily. The result was that we grew to love literature as a living occurrence and theatre as a vital art.

We also found that he didn't believe in half-measures. Whenever there was a performance by any visiting troupe of actors at the Gaiety Theatre, he obtained permission from the Headmaster and led as many as thirty of us at a time all the way into town to see a play. That is how I first saw Shakespeare's presentations, ranging from *Othello* and *Hamlet* to George Bernard Shaw's *Arms and the Man,* starring Geoffrey Kendall, Laura Liddel, Jennifer Bragg and Brian Kellet supported by the then budding thespians Shashi Kapoor, Felicity Kendall, Marcus Murch and Utpal Dutt.

For me there was another bonus that lay outside the curriculum. It was an indulgence I allowed myself and it grew with all the addiction of a secret vice. So moved was I by the revelations of 'performed literature' that I would withdraw into the dormitory when no one else was about or seek the solitude of hollows in the hillside and there I would stealthily read aloud, in many voices, from a book of poetry or prose. I would feel the onomatopoeia of words with all the sensuality of a caress and the clash of characters in conflict with all the resonance of pain and remorse and guilt. I strove to hone my voice into an instrument worthy of conveying, without apparent effort but with fluent versatility, every nuance and inflection of heart and mind. I was my only audience but I was determined to thrill me and, sometimes, to scare the hell out of myself.

Mr Asrani, was of course, totally unaware that I had turned his virtues into my vice. One day, however, quite by chance the whole school was given a glimmer of my hidden persona.

In retrospect, I think the weather had much to do with it. Himalayan winters are, to say the least, pretty cold. It was that perishing time of year when I just couldn't go out and sit in windblown hollows. Nor had I been able to find an untenanted dormitory where I could give vent to my accustomed form of release. Thus, pent up and starved for catharsis, I sat among three hundred and fifty boys in the school hall attending some function but really aware only of the distance between my chair and the warmth of the charcoal fires burning in the grates.

Suddenly, for some obscure reason that I cannot now recall, members of the audience were invited to come up on stage, if any so wished, and recite a poem and tell an anecdote. I think the incentive offered was points towards the annual Cock House shield which was as keenly sought as the Victor Ludorum cup on the sports field.

Various boys were cajoled and badgered into going up. There, in turn, they stood about limply and mumbled and returned, with obvious relief, to the refuge of their seats. No one thought of asking me. No one even glanced at me conspiratorially. My secret was safe; I had not shared it with anyone. But something within impelled me to break out of my accustomed rectitude and shyness. To my horror, I found myself standing up. Unmindful of the utter lack of cheering supporters, I walked towards the arena which others had dreaded and shirked.

Silence greeted my appearance on stage. Slowly and softly, in tune with the freezing weather outside, I evoked the atmosphere of a well-known poem by John Keats:

St Agnes Eve! Ah, bitter chill it was!
The owl for all his feathers was acold.
The hare limp'd trembling through the frozen grass
And silent was the flock in woolly fold...

As I progressed through the other stanzas, the audience seemed to shiver palpably and I'm sure I heard some teeth chattering. The rendering was rewarded with wholehearted applause – a form of appreciation I had never received before.

After the applause died away, no one thought I had worked for it. They looked upon it as a fluke, a one-off happenstance that I could not possibly repeat. It was as if I was the eleventh man in to bat and my accidental string of sixers didn't make me eligible for captaincy of the cricket team. They gave me a nod of approval but not one of recognition.

Even Mr Asrani seemed to think the brief sparkle of my foray forward was a flash-in-the-pan. He continued to look for diamonds elsewhere.

Certainly, he took us by surprise on the day of the boxing finals. Just as we were returning from the gymnasium where the matches had been in progress, he swooped down onto the path and stood firmly blocking the way. The stream of babbling schoolboys welled into a little pool before him. It seemed as if Mr Asrani wanted to congratulate those who had won their boxing colors that day. He held up his hand for silence. Then, to everyone's delight he said, "I need a volunteer who has the courage to represent the school at short notice."

The best boxers surged forward. Bishop Cotton School was well-known not only in Simla but well beyond the Himalayan foothills for its sporting spirit and manly pursuits. If there was a fight ahead, every boy wanted to be in it to prove his mettle.

I was not sure how I felt. I was the youngest and littlest of the seniors having been the recipient of a triple promotion as a junior in another school. That seeming reward for academic ability had resulted in my being permanently disadvantaged among my peers in terms of shape and size. At fourteen I felt stunted because I was small and skinny and had as yet no hair on my upper lip. In contrast, my classmates stood inches taller.

They were, on average, eighteen years old and as hirsute and muscled as mountain yaks. No wonder they called me 'mouse'.

That afternoon had been particularly painful for me. I had been badly battered and bruised in the boxing ring. My nose was swollen, my eye was shutting and, though I had fought as gamely as any finalist within reach of winning his boxing colors, I had lost the bout and all I wanted to do was to go silently into the dark of the dormitory and perhaps die.

At that point, the literature master dropped a bomb. "I need a volunteer," he clarified, "to represent the school later this evening in an all-India inter-institutional elocution competition. As you all know, a fortnight ago, I had selected a team of two but one of the boys, Kaura One, has suddenly fallen ill."

Everyone groaned and took two steps back. Someone remarked that Kaura One had been cradling an onion in his armpit for the last two days and it had worked, giving him a fever in the nick of time and sending him into hospital. No one wanted to go on stage and make a speech. It was a prospect more scary than being blown from a cannon.

Worse, the speech had to be made in front of, and in competition with, girls and boys from all over India and the venue was St Bede's – a women's college. It's not that girls were scoffed at or belittled. On the contrary, they were the stuff of dreams, gossamer creatures from another sphere, delicate hopes of happiness that hung from heaven requiring arts of communication unknown to us.

In a boys-only school, thoughts of girls are bred under a blanket and kept there. Anyone who has spoken with a girl – not his mother or sister – has spoken with an angel and thus committed sacrilege. He has crossed the area reserved to men and ventured beyond mortality to paradise. He is a Prometheus stealing fire from the gods, a task too awesome to be contemplated.

The literature master's spectacled gaze was shriveling taller boys into retreat. Two weeks ago, he had chosen the tallest – Paul Tonk and Kaura One – and now he had been let down by one of them. He obviously felt it was time to change his perspective or his philosophy. Nevertheless, he did point to one or two who stood a head above the crowd but they made quick excuses.

With an hour to go and little time to prepare, leave alone shower and change, the literature master had to settle for the least or less. Lowering his gaze he looked at me and said, "You, mouse. You. Yes. Step forward. Volunteer for the school, dammit! All you have to do is not let the side down. Just go up there. We'll be cheering you on. And deliver Kaura One's speech. It's all written out and ready. The poor bugger has been working on it for two weeks. Now go and bathe. Then get into school tie and blazer and see me in the library in twenty minutes."

Twenty minutes later, I found I couldn't read the speech. It wasn't that the handwriting was illegible, it was just that the sentences were so orotund and mellifluous that I couldn't understand what they were saying. I couldn't get a grip on the substance. I might as well have been reading Swinburne's poetry.

"Sir," I said, "I can't understand what it's about."

"About?" He seemed aghast. "You're saying that about a speech written by the chap who won the school literary prize! It's about re-structuring the United Nations Organisation, that's what it's about! It's the most popular of the subjects on the list." He was getting apoplectic and spitting in all directions.

I squirmed and mumbled, "Couldn't I speak on a less popular choice of subject? That way I wouldn't be up against too much competition and whatever I say may still sound fresh and interesting." His eyes lit up. Circles of comprehension seemed to radiate from the thick lenses of his glasses. "You mean, everyone's busy improving the UN or changing the world but you'd rather speak simply and directly about something you know, like how to cross the street safely?"

I couldn't tell whether he was being sarcastic. And there was no time to argue. He was already scanning the list of topics and the numbers of entries. "Hmm," he murmured, "six for this, five for that... Ah! This is amazing. There's actually one topic that no one has chosen. Now then, my dear mouse, that is the subject you shall speak on."

I looked over his shoulder and almost collapsed as I read, "My Ideal Wife." He seemed to be smirking in anticipation of my discomfiture.

"Right then, sir," I said, pretending nonchalance, "there's not much research I can do in the library on that subject. I'll just have to prepare a speech out of my head."

He didn't seem very happy about that. "Quotations help," he said. "Go and ask the boys if they've got any material on women."

I ran to the dorms and came back with a handful of pin-up magazines.

"Are you trying to be funny?" he gritted.

"No, sir. Seriously," I said, "here's Marilyn Monroe on the cover of this one. She's getting married."

"Again?" he groaned.

"But this time to Arthur Miller the playwright, one of America's leading intellectuals."

"Look here, mouse," he interrupted me, "I don't care what kind of a fool you make of yourself. Just don't let the school down." He flapped his arms up and down like a bat in despair and flew away.

By the time we reached the venue, the hall was packed. The doors and windows were jammed with those who couldn't get in. I crept into one of the chairs reserved for speakers on the stage.

In quick succession, the speakers spoke. Girl followed boy followed boy followed girl in a kind of molten blur. The captain of our school team Paul Tonk – more familiarly known as Tall Ponk – stood up when his turn came and opened his mouth, blushed bright red, closed it again and opened it but no sound issued forth. He had forgotten the first words of his memorized speech. As a result he couldn't say anything. He sat down. A kind of funeral pall descended over the proceedings. The evening seemed dead.

But actually it was only asleep for, towards the end, when it came my turn and I rose to speak, jittery and nervous and uncertain, my opening words – to my own amazement – seemed to kick awake that resting beast and it began to hoot and scream with unexpected, uncontrollable laughter.

All I said was, "Ladies and gentlemen, everyone dreams of an ideal... husband or wife *(A wave of surprised titters swept the audience)*. Even those who are already married *(A roar of laughter)*. But let me tell you straightaway, I don't want a woman I would have to *fight* over. As you can see from my swollen nose and black eye, I have already been badly beaten in the boxing ring today *(A wave of hilarity)*. However, I don't mind considering prospective candidates with the attributes of say, Jane Russell or Marilyn Monroe *(A gust of merriment)*. Deep thinking men tend to spread themselves thin when it comes to women *(A big belly laugh)*. After all, Arthur Miller did *(An explosion of mirth)*. He's marrying Marilyn Monroe *(Applause)*. That gentleman there seems unhappy about it *(Screams, as everyone looks to see who is being referred to)*. Perhaps he was hoping to get there first *(A howl of joy)*. No, no, not that one. I mean, the bald one over there *(A crescendo of laughter as various bald men duck in their seats)*. They say all men dream of fantastic women. I wonder what he dreams of. Or he. Or he. Or he *(Wave upon wave of laughter)*. Dare we conjecture? And do we know why?"

And so I moved on to the crux of my talk which was really about the universal human need for tenderness and understanding. At every progression of thought, it looked as though the nuns in the audience were crossing themselves while holding their sides, and the gentlemen were guffawing while roaring for more. I could see our school's rather plump Hospital Sister trying not to shriek so much with laughter; she kept stuffing a handkerchief in her mouth. This resulted in various sounds exploding from other parts of her anatomy. I felt like Androcles and the lion – the audience was eating out of my hand. It was a new experience for me. In my heart I thanked Mr Asrani for introducing me to such magic.

Ashvini Kumar, the legendary top cop of India at that time, was the chief judge and in announcing that I was being awarded not only the first prize but the team trophy because I had, single-handedly, outstripped the points won by the entire teams of the participating institutions, he used three French phrases which have remained embedded in my memory. He said, "This young boy has tremendous *joie de vivre* and displays a *savoir faire* far beyond his years combined with the *sang froid* of a veteran."

I felt strangely humbled by all the praise (and also in need of a good French dictionary). I felt like the mouse that roared.

Suddenly I was in the limelight, and felt terribly awkward. Girls from the audience engulfed me with requests for an autograph. My hand trembled as I wrote. And in the presence of the belle of the town, who I had adored from a distance, I was still tongue-tied.

The boys bore me back to school on their shoulders singing all the while. For the first time in my life, I was their hero. I had brought home the cup, the trophy and a modicum of glory.

For myself, I began to wonder whether there was a science to the art of speaking; if so I wished I could learn to repeat the feat.

After my seemingly sudden effulgence into a flower, the literature master began to take great interest in me. He decided to polish my abilities till I became a reflection of his hopes. Though he was himself a charming, pigeon-chested, lovable wreck of a human being, he insisted that I develop the physique and lung-power to speak, conversationally and casually, from one mountain peak to another. We didn't have far to go to find mountains. We were already in the Himalayas. He merely led me out, set me on a mountain top, went down into the valley himself and waited to hear me read out Mark Anthony's speech to the Romans.

Gradually, my chagrin changed to delight as, over the weeks, reading out various speeches over and around the humps of mountains, I discovered that voice projection became simple if you mastered the complex art of originating the sound in what Indian yogis call *pranayama* and the Japanese martial artists call *hara* and the Chinese Taoists call the seat of *chi*. In short, the soul of the matter lay in the lower abdomen.

So much for resonance and the generation of powerful sound. Then came the necessity to articulate it properly not only for correct enunciation but projection over distance. Mr Asrani told me how the famous Greek orator Demosthenes had trained himself to speak clearly despite holding pebbles in his mouth. That was so frightening a prospect that I quickly made sure I spoke with utmost clarity and warmth of tone.

We discussed rhetoric and mimesis; we analyzed the components of effective vocal communication and arrived at methods and principles. We created exercises. I did them. He watched. He explained that, at his age, just the theory was enough to tire him. And that is how he trained me into a warrior for the battlefields to which he led me. Of these there were many.

We always returned laden with trophies. But Mr Asrani's legacy of practical research into this old skill gave me a new learning that continues to yield benefits. I don't know where he is today or whether he is still alive. I would love to tell him all that has happened since because of what he taught me and the vistas he opened up.

Speaking well requires you to be comfortable not only with others but also with yourself, and that entails constant awareness. As Shakespeare's King Lear says, "Mend your speech a little, lest it may mar your fortunes."

By helping me mend my speech, Mr Asrani opened my mind to treasures more scintillating than might be found in Ali Baba's cave. My greatest joy today is to share these with others.

Principal Lesson

K S Venkatachalam

There are instances in our lives when certain people, especially teachers by their deeds, leave an indelible and lasting impression.

The story relates to my friend, who in the 1960s had won a government scholarship to study in a prestigious school, popularly known as the 'Eton of the East'. This school, then, was an exclusive preserve of children of the princely families, and my friend, who came from a humble background, had to struggle hard to find a place amongst the exalted. The Principal of the school, a British, who had stayed back in India after independence, was a legendary educationist. A disciplinarian, he was a strong believer in the adage 'spare the rod and spoil the child'.

Once, during the annual sports meet, the housemaster wanted both his senior and junior teams to win the inter-school football championship. He decided to include the reserve players of his senior team in the junior team. My friend, captain of the senior team, questioned the correctness of his decision which was contrary to the values cherished by the school. The housemaster, afraid of being found out, twisted the facts and complained to the Principal that my friend was instigating the students to desist from participating in the tournament.

The Principal who was extremely fond of my friend, without any forewarning caned him. My friend, who respected both his housemaster and the Principal, did not know how to react at this unexpected turn of events. He decided not to speak out against his housemaster, but was devastated by the Principal's action. A week later, the Principal came to know about the true story and called my friend to his office and, after handing over the cane to him, demanded that he be caned in return. This was his way of expressing repentance.

Later, another scholar, who is presently a top cop in Mumbai, and known for taking several bold initiatives against the underworld, had once misplaced his blazer. He was terribly upset with the loss, as he could not afford to buy another one. The Principal moved by his plight, bought him a blazer with his own money and made sure that his gesture remained a secret. The incident showed the other facet of the great man.

A few years ago, when my friend, who had himself become the Principal of a public school, came to know that his ex-housemaster was on his deathbed, he decided to pay him a visit. On seeing him, the housemaster was overcome with emotions and begged his forgiveness for the incident. Such is the mettle of great teachers.

The Write Angle

Cyprian D'Souza

I grew up in a small farming village near Mangalore in Karnataka. When I was growing up our village had no electricity, no phones, no cars and of course no television. The village certainly had something that is far more important than any of the above. We had a good school. When I studied there it was only a primary school – up to seventh standard. Now the same school has grown into a college with boarding facilities for both boys and girls.

As far as I was concerned our school was indeed the best school around. I used to look forward to going to school everyday.

The building was old ... close to a hundred years old. Classes V to VII were housed in a large hall with free standing wooden partitions. The reading room was on the stage at one end of this hall. The roof was very high. Bats and spiders, with their cobwebs, were resident in the high roof. The homing pigeons would 'coo' through the class.

The teachers, however, were young in their outlook and committed to good education.

Among all the teachers we had, I want to highlight Mr Anantharam. He taught us Kannada.

He walked barefoot everywhere. I do not think he ever owned a pair of sandals. A white dhoti, a simple white shirt and his trademark Gandhi cap completed his attire. He respected time and was scrupulously punctual. I do not know how he managed to be on time, given the fact that he walked the distance wherever he went.

All of us children were in awe of his knowledge of Old Kannada and Modern Kannada literature. He found creative ways to teach us grammar. He had great respect for Sanskrit He never missed an opportunity to show us how the structure of Indian languages arising out of Sanskrit was so rational that there was no ambiguity what so ever. In his class the students used to sit mesmerized. We absorbed every word he uttered.

Most letters of the alphabet in Kannada have a circular part to it. When they are written well with correct proportions, they look beautiful.

Part of his teaching involved undoing what we had learned. This was particularly true when it came to writing. He would have us write each letter of the alphabet in a particular way so that it was absolutely perfect. Of course for him, it was never perfect! Only close to perfect, so more practice. For most of us, learning to write correctly was a frustrating exercise as it involved breaking old habits.

Not only did we have to write the letters in a particular way, there were lessons on how to sharpen the pencils and how to hold them correctly between our fingers while writing. Most of us press the pencil or the pen on the paper especially when the assignment is difficult. The more tense we are the more leads break. When one turns to a new page in the notebook there are plenty of impressions from the previous page! He changed that pattern. We learned how to write in such a way that the pencil or pen flowed smoothly and gently while writing, without leaving any impression on the next page.

All pencils had to be sharpened well for each class. We didn't have any sharpeners (we used to call them 'cutters') instead we had to use a blade or a knife. Blades left small cuts on our fingers. The cuts never bothered us much. We respected him and wanted his approval and worked to have our pencils sharpened just right. Any approval from Mr Anantharam was a step closer to heaven.

For those of you who are curious to know how to hold the pencil correctly here it is: hold the pencil between your thumb and the index finger, resting on the middle finger as always. When writing do not bend the thumb (many do) or the index finger! Keep both the fingers as straight and relaxed as possible. Notice how gently the pencil or a pen glides on the paper. The writing angle is also important! This needs to be adjusted according to the instrument being used.

I believe a teacher makes immense contribution to an individual's life. We often forget the specific information we learned, but we carry with us the values and the attitude to life which get instilled in us. Here are the souvenirs I treasure from my Kannada teacher:

Learn the process correctly, attain perfection

Improve upon what looks perfect

Elegance is in simplicity

Each one of us finds ourselves in many situations where we are teachers. Awareness out of which we prepare and fulfill those responsibilities will determine the quality of the interactions and the depth of impact we make on the lives we touch.

A Lesson Learnt by Heart

Ratna Khemani

Today as I recall, my teachers float towards me from the past like a beautiful and memorable dream. Each taught me something precious, something worthwhile, which I've tried to pass on to my students in full measure. As I write about them, I'm forced to recollect the lines from George Bernard Shaw's poem that my father once wrote in my diary: *'Life is no mean candle for me. It is a torch which I must make burn as brightly as I can before passing it on to others.'*

I grew up in Coimbatore, where my father, a conservator of forests, was heading the Forest Research Institute. I would relish the cool, quiet, cultured flavor of this small town as I drove every day to the St Francis Convent. Managed by the Irish nuns of the Missionaries of Mary, the most predominant factor in my childhood and growing up years, was the tremendous amount of love, trust, confidence and encouragement that I received from both my parents and all my teachers.

Today when all these things are scarce, I realise what a privileged childhood it was. An enormous amount of space, quiet, greenery and nature added to my blessings. Undoubtedly, it was my father who took to tutoring me with the basics of life. Stimulating me with his stories of childhood and other world luminaries that he had interacted with, he encouraged me with his words everyday. It was in his heartening conversations that I braced myself to the feelings of dejection and disappointment that I would face one day.

But, school was a completely different ball game. It was Miss E Davie, my class teacher and English teacher in Std VII, who with her phonation introduced me to the world of poetry. Pictures came alive when she narrated excerpts from Thomas Hardy's *Woodlanders* and *Jude the Obscure* or Rudyard Kipling's *Tiger, Tiger*. Miss Davie had a beautiful handwriting; I did not. My handwritten scripts would drive her round the bend. What she couldn't understand was how could someone be so lackadaisical about improving. While I thought that it was simply not worth my effort when there were better things to do. Reading for instance, singing, dancing, playing, debating, and acting, among others. Why should I sit and slog over my handwriting, when my grades seemed to be over the top. Not the kind to give up, Miss Davie persevered and prompted and offered incentives of extra marks. Today as I watch scripts flow out of my pen, I inwardly thank this teacher for her belief in me.

I can picture Miss Gwendoline Dias' handsome face as she cycled into the school campus. Our physical training teacher, Miss Dias, a perfectionist to the core, was my special favourite. Her taut frame wouldn't deflect even as she inspected our uniform and watched us march in unison, into a perfect file. A minute late for PT meant five rounds of the oval. And yet, we all respected and adored her. If I won a trophy for the school, I did it because of the faith she had in me. I could not let Miss Dias down. Today when I teach confidence-building at management institutes and elsewhere, I admit to borrowing heavily from the practical lessons that I learnt from her.

Miss Mallika was Head of the Department of Mathematics, at the Nirmala College in Coimbatore – also run by nuns, but of the presentation convent order. A corollary to my affinity for

Maths and Physics was my love for NCC parades possibly because of Miss Mallika, who was also a NCC officer. Born with an affinity for facts and figures and a natural flair for quick solutions for sines, cosines, theorems and differentials, this aptitude was compounded by the fine teaching methods of Miss Mallika. Eventually, I went on to top the university in Mathematics and Physics. But it was the *masala dosa* breakfasts after the parade with Miss Mallika that I recall fondly. Bent on proving her right, I later went on to win the President's gold medal for being the best all India NCC cadet.

Today when someone asks me; Are you a teacher? I sum up with Shaw's quote. *"I'm not a teacher: only a fellow-traveller of whom you asked the way. I pointed ahead—ahead of myself as well as you."* It's a lesson I ask my students to learn by heart.

Turning Point

Padmaja P Godbole

I had just passed my eleventh standard (SSC) from D E Society's Dravid High School, Wai and was dreaming of going to Pune to join my two older brothers to pursue further studies. But it was not to be! My father used to suffer from heart palpitations and this made him think that he would die soon. Like all fathers, he wanted to get me married off so that he didn't have to worry about me in case of his untimely death. I was devastated when I heard of this decision of his.

Mr G M Joshi, the then headmaster of Dravid High School, Wai was a good friend of my father's. When he heard that I was going to be made to discontinue my studies he came to our house. He spoke with my father and managed to convince him that I must have some kind of higher qualifications to make me stand on my own feet. He suggested that I should go to Pune to do the Secondary Teacher's Certificate (STC). He told him that as it was only a year's course, it was unlikely that my father would die in that period. Coincidentally, Mr Joshi was transferred to the New English School, Ramanbaug where I had taken admission for STC. Naturally my father requested him to become my local guardian and mentor. At the time of my final examinations, he suggested to the examiner to test me thoroughly as he said, "She is my star student and is a *khankhanit banda rupaiya*" (a rupee coin that will ring true)! Those words still ring in my ears.

Along with the STC Exam, I had also appeared for the First Year Arts examination as an external student as I wanted to make the most of my being in Pune. My close friend Lesia Sathe who was a regular student of SP College helped me to study with the help of her notes. I somehow got through with a Pass (Third) class. At the same time, I cleared my STC exam with a distinction.

Mr Joshi and my elder siblings congratulated me for my 'sterling' determination as they described it. They convinced my father to let me continue my studies. He conceded.

Mr Joshi always had a peaceful and quiet approach even to our mischief in his class. For example, I never liked my drawing classes; so I used to make funny faces as soon as the teacher's back was turned towards the class. The whole class would laugh. Eventually one day, I got caught while doing this. I was asked to leave the classroom at once and go and tell the principal what I had done and then to wait outside his office. So I did what I was told and kept standing outside his office for a long time. Perhaps Joshi Sir had forgotten about me altogether. I was feeling nervous because I was going to miss the next period too, when I suddenly sighted Mr Joshi coming towards me. In the manner that teachers could use in those days, he told me, "I am just now writing to the local circus owner. He is willing to hire you. Would you like to go? You seem to be good at it (clowning)." I knew what he meant. I apologised and was sent back to the class.

Mr Joshi taught English and Mathematics. He used to make his classes very interesting. He never had to demand good behavior or discipline of his students. He used to command it because of his nature and excellent rapport with the students. The whole school respected and loved this great person.

To me, Mr Joshi was like a precious stone, a rare gem. He was the catalyst that changed the direction of my life and indirectly raised my father's sinking morale. He made me into the strong person that I am today. The investment that he made in me made me what I am today. I hold the BA, MEd degrees and a postgraduate diploma from Canada in the education of exceptional children and run a full fledged school for exceptional children in Pune. This, for a 16 year old girl from Wai whose academic ambitions would have ended with marriage, is indeed a memorable journey. With all the humility at my command, let me say, "Thank you, Joshi Sir, I owe you everything."

Indebted for a Lifetime

P S Palande

Like any student, I was influenced by many teachers and learnt something or the other from each one of them. Some were instrumental in improving my handwriting, while some others inspired me to learn Sanskrit, Hindi, English and other languages. Some teachers initiated me into the techniques of acquiring general knowledge, while some others impressed upon me the importance of adopting certain values in life.

But there are some whose influence pervades a student's life on a long term basis and over a broad canvas. I always think of at least two of them who have had a profound influence on my life. Acknowledging the debt of just two teachers should not be construed to mean that I underrate the others. It only suggests that their impact on my life has been deeper.

The first is Mr M L Patwardhan, affectionately and popularly known to all as 'Anna', who was my teacher in the Modern High School, Pune. 'Anna' was the one who went much beyond the textbooks and persuaded us to take an interest not just in academic matters, but also in extra-curricular activities. He was the one who tried to turn his students into all-rounders. Apart from teaching us specific subjects, he spent considerable time teaching us many other subjects including Dnyaneshwari! Most of these extra inputs were given to us outside the normal school hours, on the school playground! Frankly, it was not his responsibility to do it, but he used to do so out of affection for his students.

He used to insist that we should all assemble at the playground every evening and participate in all the games. These activities brought immense benefit to us, which we did not realize at that young age. Had it not been for him, many would not have discovered their latent talent in sports like hockey, athletics, indigenous Indian games and gymnastics. He himself was a good sportsman and could teach us most games.

What is more important here however is that he made us imbibe true sportsmanship, a quality, which is sadly lacking in many sportsmen today. A true Scout, he inculcated in us very many other qualities, which stood us in good stead in later life. In an effort to help us develop our personality, he even went to the extent of guiding us in small things such as how to stand erect, how to walk, how to talk, how to study and many other things. I feel my personal development owes a lot to his teaching. I can, without any reservation, assert that he was certainly one of the main architects of my career.

It is a wonder that he could persuade us to stay on the ground till late in the evening. He knew each one of us and our families well. Anna endeared himself to us so much that we were never under any pressure when we interacted with him. He was so easy to get along with. Anna's abiding interest in the welfare of his students is what probably keeps him young and energetic even today when he is eighty! In fact, it is almost fifty years since we left Modern High School; yet many of us still are in contact with him. He is as cheerful as ever and enjoys meeting us. We had a gathering of Modern's Past Students recently and as was to be expected, it was Anna who was most in demand and who was all the time surrounded by his former students!

The other teacher whom I always recall with great fondness is the famous Professor G P Pradhan. He had an equal influence on my personal development. He mildly but effectively conveyed to me in the very first year in college that I needed to work harder to acquire proficiency in English. But he did not stop at merely tendering his advice. He took personal interest in me to the extent that I think it would have been embarrassing to ignore his advice!

I remember our first meeting in the Fergusson College Library when he inquired about my interests in life and about what I read. He then gave me some tips on how to read a book and how to distill the essence of it. He followed this up with lending me about five or six books from the library with a suggestion that I should meet him again in the library after a week or so. When I met him again, he inquired about my impression of the books. I was delightfully vague. After some questioning, he knew I had not read them. Surprisingly, without losing his temper, he asked me to take home the same books again and come back after I felt confident about discussing the contents of the books.

I had no alternative but to read the books carefully before I met him a third time. This was a turning point and from then onwards I developed a passion for reading and making notes, and more importantly, improving my vocabulary. He expressed satisfaction with my progress and gave instructions to the library staff to lend me any book that I wanted – a rare privilege for a college student. I must say I utilized it fully. Professor Pradhan also persuaded me to write a few essays, which he read with great care and corrected along with me.

But something more was to come. On one occasion he asked me to be present for a debate competition, and without informing me suddenly announced my name as the next speaker. He made me pick up a chit for an extempore speech; the subject that I happened to pick up was "If I were the College Queen!"

That was the first time that I had made a speech, but to my surprise, I was adjudged the best speaker! That inflated my ego, but in retrospect I guess that he had given me a good rating, not so much for my performance, but perhaps to encourage me. It did help.

Professor Pradhan used to illustrate how words (such as joy, pleasure, happiness, satisfaction), which are often used as synonyms, actually conveyed different shades of meaning. He took great pains to explain the nuances of oratory and helped me overcome stage fright. Then for three or four years in a row, I bagged several prizes in debate competitions at the inter-collegiate level and was elected the Debating Secretary of the College.

I have no words to acknowledge the contribution of both Mr Patwardhan and Professor Pradhan to my career. In particular, my success in the UPSC examination with such flying colours was possible owing to the efforts they made to shape my personality. The beauty of it was that although each was formally a teacher of a given subject, they taught the students far beyond that. In fact, even more than the basic academic inputs, they excited in us an interest in the varied departments of life in a very subtle way.

Both impressed their students with their simplicity, though they never formally uttered a word about it, nor did they ever read out a sermon extolling the virtues of a simple life. Or again, both of them were so straightforward in word and deed that one just could not but be impressed by that transparency. Their commitment to their profession was so apparent, yet they never boasted of it. They simply conveyed the importance of these aspects of one's personality by their own example. These were the qualities which many of their students imbibed almost unconsciously and which help them reap rich dividends in life.

It is with great gratitude that I place on record their contribution to the enrichment of my mind and my whole life.

Sister Superior: Above Par
Gayatri Chatterjee

When I went to study at Sophia Convent I understood but could not speak English. Ironically, the very first class I attended the day I joined (in Class VIII) had Mrs Seymore teaching *As You Like It*. She walked to and fro as she read, gesticulating as if she were some thespian Shakespearean actor on stage. I was fascinated by her histrionics and the open discussions on romantic love in class. Towards the end she asked me a question and I stood up mum. The girls cried in unison, "Miss, she does not understand English." "What rubbish!" she boomed, "I saw she understood me perfectly well – perhaps even better than some of you did." And she dragged me to the Principal, Sister Yvonne, wanting to coach me privately. The Sister mused, "But her parents might not want an additional expenditure ..." (My joining a convent school and boarding had been a big jump in all ways for the entire family). Mrs Seymore put an end to the matter by saying she was going to teach me for free. It was a few months before my father got to know of this and began paying her.

This story actually is about Sister Yvonne, the Principal – Sister Superior to us. A principal gathers around her a body of exemplary teachers, sets the environment of a school. To speak about her is to speak about other teachers too. In the first exams

I took in Sophia, I found two sums had been wrongly set (I remember one had to do with square root). So I called for the maths teacher Gita Benette. Initially she did not believe me but then she got involved; she sat besides me (in the exam hall), discussed the sums – and replaced them with other sums. We have always remained good friends.

Sister Yvonne – our sister Superior – was an amazing personality and I loved her with all the passion of a first love. I was told about the 'crush' that girls have over teachers and elder students. Sister, more than any pedestrian psychologist could, understood such love and could channel it in various directions without destroying it. All students benefited differently from that 'channeling'.

She was a severe disciplinarian and we greatly feared her. At times she supported those who broke rules. Sister Victoria, for instance, could any time interrupt studies and take me along for her social service in the city.

Sister Superior loved cinema and got a nun trained in running the projector – I first saw *Bicycle Thieves* in the Sophia hostel. Once a year, filled in army buses, we would visit Delhi under some pretext (like donating money to the Prime Minister's Fund for some noble cause); and then we would see a film. Once the Hindi teacher was allowed to take me (a Bengali) to a Sunday show of Tapan Sinha's *Atithi*, because the film was an adaptation of a Tagore story and it was my birthday.

We had catechism for one year. One day in the class, a Sister was teaching us about the apocalypse. Madhu Kapoor stood up to say, "Sister, we too have stories about the world coming to an end"; the sister reacted in a knee-jerk fashion and spewed out a – "What rubbish!" Some of us stood up and informed her that different religious texts can have similar motifs and explanations to things. The nun walked out angrily.

Supper in the hostel was at 7.00 pm and then followed the 'Grand Silence'. We settled down to study, the nuns went to the chapel, and Sister Superior used the interim half-an-hour for talking over serious matters with the older girls. That night she explained to us, "Not all of us come here because this is *the* vocation; not all of us have heard God's call. Some are here for other reasons, for example, poverty. Big families often send their young ones to be a priest or a nun; some escape here for free food, shelter and security. Please learn to treat them with compassion."

And while at Grand Silence, I am reminded of a time when I was living in one room, and my two children studying at St Mary's and Bishop's, Pune, would come home on weekends and all holidays. Imagine two young kids in a ten by twelve! I had instituted a rule of silence after dinner, when we all did our own stuff before sleep. My children remember those hours as among the most precious times of their childhood.

I attended the entire Catholic calendar one full year and there was a rumor that I was going to convert. I approached Sister Superior; she asked me, "Do you want to embrace Christianity?" I said, "No". At once she snapped, "Then why are you bothered about what others say?"

She would take Moral Science lessons for Class X and we were discussing 'sex'. I asked, "Sister, I understand the sexual act can be pleasurable; but why use the term 'ecstasy?'" She quipped, "How should I know, I have never done it." Some days later, she said, "How can the girls benefit from such cloudy, flowery knowledge of sex?" She introduced sex education for us – I don't know how many schools in the sixties did that.

We mingled with the city people at local fairs and *melas*. That year I was preparing for my ICSC and had stayed away from all diversions. She came to me quite distraught. And confided; "The girls were seen behaving (at the mela) in such giddy-headed fashion". I told her, "Sister, I have mixed with boys since my infancy; but many of these girls have never talked to a boy let alone do things." She rushed to Delhi and arranged for a 'dance' with the boys of St Xaviers.

Sister Yvonne had come to Pune once when I was already here with my family. I met her and the first thing she told me was, "You know, I have undertaken psychoanalysis and it is so fantastic. One comes to know so much about one's own self." She came home for dinner and I realized with a shock that the woman who stood for me as the source of so much of wisdom, moral and ethical courage had been only thirty-five when I had come into association with her.

The Art of Conquering Numbers
Nalini Swamidasan

She was young. When we were 14 or 15 years old, she was just 19. Mavis Mathais had only completed her first year in science at college when she came to teach us mathematics in the pre-matriculation class. That was fifty-nine years ago at St Teresa's Convent, Santa-Cruz, Mumbai. Those were the days when schools did not always employ teachers with degrees or with teacher training diplomas. Mavis Mathias knew her subject and loved it so much that she got everyone to understand it and to love it too.

At St Teresa's of that time, maths was not a subject that girls excelled in. Maths was generally looked upon as a masculine subject. However it was also believed that 'Hindu' girls managed to do well in it. What I am particularly grateful to Miss Mathias for is the self-confidence that she developed in us. I was fond of maths and was fairly good at it. But she made us excel in it. No problem was beyond one's capacity, no subject was difficult. One had just to apply oneself and put in concentrated effort to excel in a subject.

Miss Mathias's enthusiasm for maths was infectious. She came to school armed with additional problems taken from textbooks other than those prescribed for us. She assigned us massive amount of homework everyday and the problems set were so many that a large majority in the class worked only for maths. Girls sat with maths even during lunch break and some of us who were good in the subject helped those who were a little deficient.

These maths-oriented efforts caught the attention of the other teachers who began to complain that the class neglected all other subjects. Down came the headmistress of the school and the Mother Superior to advise the girls about the need to value all subjects and of the importance of an all-round development, etc. The homework and the barrage of problems in maths continued nevertheless and so did the excitement of finishing the homework. Miss Mathias's hold on the class was complete. We had all begun to love her in spite of her being a hard task master. She was friendly and approachable. She was a very good communicator and maths became very simple in her hand. She made great demands on our time and attention but we were only too willing to fulfill them.

Such devotion and love for a subject is rare to come by. Over the years I have come to realize that what one needs in a teacher, especially at the school level, is not high academic qualifications but this enthusiasm for the subject taught and the desire and capacity to communicate clearly. In today's Mumbai, Mavis Mathias would have been too young and of course not qualified to teach the two highest classes in the school. The rapport she had with the class, the complete attention she commanded are experiences I can never forget. She became my model of a good teacher.

The maths class was also the ground for character training. Those who were good in maths were inspired with a desire to scale to more difficult heights. "To follow knowledge like a sinking star, beyond the utmost bound of human thought" (To quote Tennyson's *Ulysses*). For those who were weak, it was sheer practice, solving problems over and over again. Finally, we were a class with many securing a distinction in maths at the matric exam and no failures in maths.

At college, I took mathematics in the first year but curiosity to learn a new subject and destiny beckoned me to Logic at the Intermediate Arts. It is not what I did with maths in my later life but what maths under Miss Mathias did to me, to my person that is significant. Maths became sheer fun and it strengthened the belief in myself, in my capacity to master any subject I chose. A good teacher like Mavis Mathias is one who ignites a spark in her students, a spark of excitement and great love for the subject. She is one who spurs all students to put in maximum efforts; to be strong in will, 'to persevere and achieve one's goal'.

When Teachers Become Friends
Nandita Saikia

In a way, one of the greatest gifts any teacher can give a student, I think, is to inculcate a curiosity to learn.

I've been incredibly lucky to have at least one such teacher at every stage in my life. The first was Mrs Rowlands who taught me in primary school. She taught me to read without ever pushing me. She made me want to read more by giving me some of the most interesting children's books available. And although I still love to go back to those books from time to time, it was only because of her that I was able to read Shakespeare by the time I was ten, and Chaucer a year later.

In later years, it was Mr A N Patil, my Marathi and Hindi Teacher who made a huge impression on me. Every lesson he took, was spiced with half a dozen or more anecdotes from a wide variety of subjects: among them history, politics, religion and sociology. I was, and still am in awe of his knowledge, which despite rather desperate attempts, I doubt I'll ever be able to match.

There have also been other teachers who helped me to try to become independent: to think and act for myself using my own judgment, which to my mind has been just as, if not more important, than actually learning anything. After all, it's much too easy to become a completely useless repository of facts and little else.

Two teachers whom I remember in particular are Mrs Cynthia Nesamani and Sister Monica, both taught me in school. The former, by and large, gave me a free rein to do what I wanted to do. I, being one of those people who dislikes instructions, she helped me to produce much better results than I'd have otherwise done.

I remember her asking us in the ninth standard to make globes for our geography projects. A classmate, Ruchi Sanghvi, and I slogged for endless hours to make one, and at the end of it, I remember Mrs Nesamani telling us that it wasn't what she'd expected. For a moment, which seemed incredibly long, we were crestfallen till she clarified that the standard of our project was only expected from graduate students.

Sister Monica, however, wasn't quite as lenient as that, and spent most of the time telling me about the importance of regularity and hard work. She made me realise that success is, like genius, 99 per cent perspiration and 1 per cent inspiration. It's a lesson that has stood me in good stead.

The teachers I'm most grateful to, though, are not those who have taught me the most, but those who have simply been friends to me, believed me and believed in me. Prominent among them is Sudha Ramasubramanium – Rambo, as we used to call her. I didn't know Mrs Ramasubramanium too well. She taught me in college, and apart from being incredible in class, she also believed that I actually had a problem when I developed an injury which several doctors found difficult to diagnose, and despite my missing an exam – the HSC, of all exams – she was the only person who told me to concentrate on my health and assured me that I could take the exam off the top of my head any time I wanted to.

I'm not even certain she remembers it, but at the time, it felt like one of the only rays of hope in an extremely dark tunnel. Perhaps few teachers realise how far their influence extends or how much of a difference their actions and words can make. A number of my teachers have unfortunately taught me kindness and tolerance and patience by being precisely the opposite, and quite obviously, they aren't the people I like to think about. But many of my teachers have been extraordinary people, who have not only taught me in class but also helped mold me and my character in every other way. I only hope that I live up to what their endeavors were undoubtedly meant to create.

To Sir, with Love

S K Savanur

Several persons have influenced and guided me. They are all responsible for making me what I am today. This includes great actors, media persons, authors, spiritual leaders and several teachers.

However, I feel that among them all, it is one of my school teachers, the late Mr B S Shrikhande who has a very special place in my life. If I think of him from where I stand today, he was a very simple and ordinary man. He was just a face in the crowd, to put it candidly. He was our class teacher when I was studying in the tenth standard at the Basel Mission Higher Secondary School, Dharwad during 1964 – 65.

Mr Shrikhande taught us English and Mathematics. He taught mathematics as though he was handling a poem in English literature, as he made the complex principles in mathematics appear simple, vivid and enjoyable. At the same time, he taught the English language with the precision and logic of mathematics. I have an MSc degree in Applied Mathematics, but none of the professors at college or university level ever taught the subject as clearly as did Mr Shrikhande. I worked with the British Council for nearly sixteen years and thanks to the methods adopted by Mr Shrikhande in teaching us the English language, I always had an edge over the others.

The excellent foundation laid by Mr Shrikhande pays me rich dividends till this day.

I remember Mr Shrikhande for one more reason. During those days, on the last working day of every month school used to end at 3.30 pm, nearly two hours before the usual time. Throughout our school years we used to look forward to that day. However, during the last year of schooling, Mr Shrikhande, our class teacher, used to wait outside the classroom till the previous teacher had walked out and enter the room to tell us one precious thing. He used to say, "Today is the 30th of June. You will get many 30th Junes in your life, but not the 30th June, 1964. This is the final year of your schooling. The examinations are fast approaching. Get focused, get ready. Thank you."

He would do it month after month. Only the date, month and the year changed, but the rest of the content remained the same. He used to say these words in a calm, sincere, well-meaning and soft voice. The sense of moving time used to send shivers down our spine. It also had a great cleansing effect on us. He made us aware of the importance of time. In the process, he also showed us that he cared for us and that he understood what was going on in our minds. Even now, on the last day of every month I get charged by remembering him and his words.

My teaching style is partly influenced by Mr Shrikhande. I include a number of examples driven from common sense in all my lectures. Newspapers and other media give fresh instances to illustrate the complex ideas in my discipline. I convey many values to my students wherever it is relevant. I add all those factors, which I think, will make my students appreciate the nice things of life and enable them to make better professional decisions. I make them think afresh. I try to help them break the molds that need to be broken. Because of my teacher, Mr Shrikhande, I am sure that education does not mean answering questions, but a questioning of the answers.

Irreverently, Ever Yours

Anjali Ray

Most of us in India begin school chanting *guru Brahma, guru Vishnu, guru devam*. There's a phase in our lives when we literally hang on to the teacher's word as God's own. The adage in the primary section is "*The Teacher is always right*". Then we graduate and see our former teachers without rose tinted spectacles. Once we take them off their pedestals, we see them as what they really were – ordinary mortals with normal feelings and failings. When I tried to recall former teachers who I still remember with affection, several faces floated before my eyes. I'll describe three of them.

I was standing in the row of the about-to-enter third standard students in my missionary school at the end of the long summer break. The names of all my classmates in Section B were called out — 'Harjeet Kaur, Madhulika ...', and they stepped to another row. I waited for my name to be called. The entire class was being shepherded by their class teacher to the allotted classroom without a mention of my name. I panicked. Had I failed? Would I be left behind in second standard? How could that have happened? I had ranked third. I found myself in a group in which I did not recognise a single face except my neighbour, Jayashree's. A tall nun appeared. She had a thin, long face and she wore glasses. Sister Monica was bemused. "Is she always so quiet?" she asked Jayashree. I was mortally afraid of anyone in a nun's habit. Nuns meant rules; they meant being hit on the knuckles with wooden rulers, they meant flying dusters. But Sister Monica, despite her severe features, did not seem like the knuckle-hitting-duster-throwing sort. She reassured me, with a twinkle, that I had been assigned a different section.

Once we were in the classroom, Sister took over. Not merely maintaining our progress reports and teaching us English, which was her subject. But our entire lives ranging from hygiene and needlework to ethics and morality. And Sister Monica, unlike my former class teacher Miss Sultana, had no 'pets'. She had cast me as a number one contender though I was not light-eyed like the last year's topper Anupa Pande nor plump and cute like Alka Shah. She rewarded good work and punished bad regardless of who did it. And she involved everyone in the class discussions, even quiet ones like me.

I was curious about Sister Monica. What did her hair look like? My classmate assured me nuns were bald. Where did she go when the school closed for the vacation? When she spoke of her growing-up years she had mentioned a home. Did she still go home? She was very light-skinned but spoke fluent Hindi. Was she Indian or British? I was still unaware of the category Anglo Indian. In spite of all the lessons Sister Monica had given to make me come out of my shell, I couldn't muster the courage to ask her who she was, where she came from, and what she came for, and what she did apart from teaching us. But now I know. Without hearing the answer from her lips. She was a nun and her religion was to fashion small Indian girls into proper young women. Because she did not have a home, the whole world was her home. Because she had no children, she had everybody else's. I am not sure if I am 'propah' or not but I still cross my heart when I enter a church, I still mind my language, and I still dry my fingers before starting on my needlework.

Next, I was admitted into a Hindi-Hindu school run with great affection and efficiency by a bevy of Kumaoni singles. It was a different form of nunhood. They embraced me and inducted me into the maze of Hindi numerals. I loved all my teachers, but my personal favourite was Basanti. Basanti Rawat was not as fair and pretty as Kala didi, the universal favourite.

Nor did she sing as well as Gayyoor Fatima, the tragedy queen. But her kohl eyes flashed and her smile lit up her face. And not only in the presence of the Physical Education Master Mr Singh with whom she was allegedly in love. She made school a truly involved experience. She knew the names of everybody's mother. She remembered to put everybody's brother in the front row on their first day in school. She could talk about any subject under the sun. From dance to geography. And the months she officiated as principal before the stern *badi didi* joined were truly fun. You could sing when it rained, play *kho kho* if the teacher called sick. And the entire school joined in the Annual Day preparations. I was included in the group song even though I was tone deaf because all must participate. When I descended the steps clutching my prize for the best student, I caught Basanti didi's sweet smile. I waved her good-bye. Where are you Basanti Rawat? Or are you Mrs Singh now? I am rereading Shivani's novels set in the Kumaon hills. Perhaps Basanti is hiding somewhere in those pages.

I am officially an adult now. And a front-bench undergraduate at the capital's best women's college. A matronly woman had just waddled in a 'nylex' saree with a mismatched blouse. Malati Verma's homely figure was perfectly mismatched with her razor sharp brain and wit. Out of that slightly upturned lip erupted a stiff upper lip accent in spite of a totally un-traveled English world beginning with Charles Dickens which she taught, but could veer off in any direction from Virginia Woolf and James Joyce to V S Naipaul. The accent was new to me. I strained hard to understand. Most others claimed that not the accent but the content went above their heads. But I walked on undeterred by content and accent. And reaped the rewards at the end of my contact. I learnt about England and the English novel from A to Z.

Professor Verma stood by what she believed. She walked out of the class because a cheeky student dared to pass notes to another when she was in the midst of the most serious bit in *Oliver Twist*. The class was condemned to complete the text on their own. She left for Oxford on a fellowship. Malati Verma stomped out of Oxford six months later. Because England discriminated. I heard Oxford English in India from Malati Verma. I heard about Oxford from Malati Verma. I have always steered clear of Oxford. Into post-coloniality, into which I drag England and the rest of the world. Because teaching is like that. You can begin anywhere and end anywhere, along any route. Breaking boundaries. Next time I am in Delhi I will trace you Ms Verma. Hope you will spare time to share a few tips. On how you did it.

A Habit of Benevolence

Geeta Sundar

Saints and Gods seem far removed from reality, but there are a few human beings who influence us a great deal, leaving a lasting impression on our minds. Foremost amongst these are teachers, and the maximum impact on our minds is made by *school* teachers who have the unique opportunity to mold fresh minds into any shape they please, since their students hold them in great esteem and awe.

Sister Sylvia was one such person. She was my teacher 45 years ago, when I was five years old, and studying in the first standard. She was beautiful, fair and serene. Her face (which could break into a very sunny and lively smile), words and actions are permanently etched on my mind. She literally lived what she taught and believed in. Very much like Gandhiji. As the story goes, a mother once requested him to tell her son to stop eating salt as advised by the doctor. Gandhiji called the mother and son after 15 days so that *he* could see whether he himself was able to avoid the temptation of taking salt before talking to the child. Buddha has also said, "A man should first direct himself in the way he wants to go, before instructing others." Sister Sylvia lived by these principles.

She took her job as a nun and teacher seriously; and in the process shaped us into strong characters morally, mentally and physically. Albert Einstein has said, "It is the supreme art of the teacher to awaken joy in creative expression and knowledge." Sister knew how to impart knowledge in the most creative and joyful way possible.

Neatness and cleanliness were her first priorities. Wonderfully trim and neat herself, she checked our nails, collars, feet, hair and ears regularly. The unclean child was made to stand a few minutes in front of the whole class. Most children did not want to stand there more than once! 'Cleanliness is Godliness' was her motto, not 'Cleanliness is *next to* Godliness' and to us there was no one neater, cleaner and godlier, than Sister Sylvia.

Teaching was always made interesting. When the weather was fine, she often took us outdoors. Most of us liked her so much that we behaved ourselves even when teaching was conducted outside the classroom. A smile, a pat on the back or a caress from her was always treasured; it made our day memorable. Samuel Johnson has said, "Praise, like gold and diamonds, owes its value to its scarcity." Since she did not praise us often, any appreciation shown by her was always cherished.

She expected all of us to study hard. The lax child was wrapped in a sheet, with a dunce cap on her head and made to parade the school. Strangely, the punished child did not bear a grudge against Sister but made sure that she never repeated the mistake. One or two such instances made the whole class work like beavers.

Her proverbs and adages were always illustrated with examples so that we never forgot them. Once she told the prefect to fetch the class register from the office. When the girl came back empty handed, Sister went herself. Stepping into the class with the register she said, "When you want a job done fast, do it yourself!"

She paid equal attention to our nutrition. Once a week there would be a surprise tiffin check in the afternoon. Once I did not eat my lunch as my mother (with five kids and a job) had forgotten to put salt in the *Upma*. Sister caught me that day. When she had heard out my excuse, she told me to call my sister from the second standard with *her* tiffin. Finding that similarly full, she asked a boarder to fetch salt from the kitchen and made both of us eat in front of the class. The homily delivered that day was —"When you have a problem don't avoid it, solve it."

Once in a while the whole class was taken out for a movie. We were shown good movies like *Benhur, Ten Commandments,* and *The Sound of Music*. On the way whenever we saw a beggar or a handicapped person, Sister made us stop and thank God for not giving us any disability, and for being born into a good family. Even now when I see a handicapped person, I automatically find myself thanking God for all that He has given me.

Sister Sylvia wanted to become a doctor and I remember she left suddenly, probably to fulfill her ambition. Do nuns become doctors and can they continue to wear their habits? I do not know. We were too young for anyone to confide in us as to the reasons for her leaving our school. I am sure she found it a very small platform for her burning desire to leave a mark in this world.

I do not know where Sister Sylvia is now. But wherever she is I know she must still be influencing and inspiring many minds around her, and in the process, leaving a part of her with them to treasure, as I will always do. "Give me four years to teach children and the seed I have sown will never be uprooted", said Vladimir Lenin. The seeds sown by Sister Silvia in one year are still to be uprooted from my mind.

She was a rare combination of a good human being, an inspiring teacher and a management guru all rolled in one. Mother Teresa has said — "Let no one come to you without coming away a better and happier person." Thank you Sister Sylvia for making me a better and happier person!

No "Short Corners"

Arnavaz Damania

To be a tall and lanky girl of 12 years (now 65), and in school was terrible in those days. It meant being teased and given all sorts of names. I did not come from an affluent family. So I was a very shy and introverted girl.

I loved sports and was good at them. In fact I was one of the top sports girls of my school. Hockey was my favourite and I made quite an impact in those days with my game.

My maiden name was Arnavaz Irani. We were three sisters who played hockey. One of my sisters had the same name and surname as another hockey player. So, we sisters changed our surname to Adar from Irani to help people on the field call out to us, and to the other girl without confusion.

I always had the fascination to see the world and to meet people. Since I couldn't study further due to financial constraints (despite a sports scholarship at college), I set my heart on becoming an airhostess — the best way to travel and get paid for it! However, when I went to my Principal, Mrs Mani Bharucha of Dastur Girls' High School to get her signature on the application form, this ordinarily meek and mild person grew livid with rage to see that I had again changed my surname to Irani. At once she turned to me and asked, "When you have made a name as Adar, why do you want to change it again to

Irani?" I explained the reason. But she was not convinced. "Look ahead," she advised me, "never behind. What is behind is what you have done, so see that you do that well. There is always so much more for you in front. Choose the best and enjoy every bit of the life you have with pride."

Her words have often come back to me at different stages of my life. Mrs Bharucha was a wonderful lady who encouraged me in every way, though I dare say, she often had to send for my mother to tell her she would dismiss me! I was a very hot-headed person and though shy, would stand up for my rights. This often created a problem for my principal.

Once, because of some school politics, my sports teacher whom I admired greatly suddenly disbanded the team in which I was playing. I immediately joined the seniors' team as I was used to running with the seniors. My sports teacher ordered me to run with the junior athletes. I grew adamant and refused. Mrs Bharucha then intervened and diffused the situation. She persuaded the sports teacher to let go.

There were other times too when she helped me. This was when I would get into trouble with my academic teachers for failing to attend their special classes because of my having to participate in hockey and other tournaments for the school. Mrs Bharucha would see to it that I was let off. She was always very fair when there were complaints about me doing exactly as I pleased. She would support me against the staff if she felt I had done no wrong.

Thanks to her and some others, I am what I am today. I wish all youngsters would look ahead positively, instead of only living for today. It was a precious lesson that Mrs Bharucha taught me nearly 53 years ago.

Passing the Torch On

Ashok R Kelkar

The relationship between the taught and the teacher fascinates me. I suppose this is in part because I have enjoyed the relationship from both ends. Yes, 'enjoyed' is the word. I had a rather long innings as one taught from the Infant Class, as it used to be called those days, to the course-work followed by the writing of the thesis towards a Doctorate in Philosophy, all without much of a break and again a long innings as one teaching undergraduates, postgraduates and doctoral candidates. I can say for sure that my enjoyment was conditioned both by traditional India's conception of the relationship and the modern European conception of it. There was no sense of discontinuity or any resulting discomfort in my stint as a student, thanks to my teachers, or at least some of them. How do I know how, at a later date, my own students found me as a teacher? More of that later, first the two conceptions.

With us in traditional India, there are two key words for the teacher, *guru* and *acharya*. Earlier, both terms simply meant someone who initiates the young to the sacred ritual. In the course of history, guru came to be associated with the mysteries of the quest, whether spiritual or artistic. Guru was larger than life (guru means large after all); he was the gracious master who transmitted the torch of energy. Acharya come to be associated with the determined search for truth, whether philosophical or scientific. The acharya was the elder pathfinder; indeed he aspires to be excelled by someone he has taught (*sisyad icchet parajayam*); he was the kindly father, who initiated the dialogue (*vada-vivada*) and transmitted the torch of knowledge. We in India were content to use the same correlative for both these terms, namely, *sisya*, one to be disciplined (*siksa*) after the initiation (*diksa*). (In Islamic India, one comes across the terms *ustad* and *maulavi*, which correspond, after making due allowances, to the terms guru and acharya respectively, *sagird* being the correlative of both.) Modern Europe, on the contrary, differentiates the two kinds of the taught: pupil / *eleve* / *schuler* and student / *etudiant* / student. The pupil is the little child led by the hand by the teacher, who may be the ordinary school teacher or the eminent pathfinder among scholars. The student is one who studies diligently and systematically, whether in attendance to a teacher or simply pursuing knowledge in the footsteps of those who have taught him earlier.

A moment's thought will show that there is a certain correspondence between the Indian and the European conception: between the guru and the pupil on the one hand and again between the acharya and the student. So the two conceptions are not all that distinct, but there is a difference nevertheless. In traditional India, there is such a great weightage to the guru mode that even an acharya stands in danger of shading into the guru and so being implicitly followed. In modern Europe, one sets a higher store by the student mode so much so that even a school pupil stands in danger of being pressed into diligent and systematic study. (The malady probably spread from France to other countries.)

To reminisce about my teachers is thus for me to contemplate the emergence of a fusion mode in my own relationship with them, fusion of the guru and pupil mode and the acharya and student mode.

I was in my fourth school year, lucky to have the gifted Shri Ranade for our class teacher who taught us everything from language to sciences. In the course of a grammar lesson he inductively derived the definition of 'adjective' through example, finally inscribing it on the blackboard : An adjective (*visesana*) is a word that gives us special (*visesa*) information about the noun, as in *kala ghoda*, where the first word qualifies the noun 'horse' as 'black'. Up went a hand, my hand : "I have a problem, Sir, *kala* doesn't say anything about the noun as *don–aksari* (two-syllabled) would correctly have about the second word, *ghoda*. Maybe we should modify the definition so as to read 'special information about what the noun indicates' rather than 'about the noun' as such." Shri Ranade stopped in his tracks, thought for a minute, and actually revised the definition on the blackboard and, showing his pleasure, said, "You're right, of course." Needless to say, my admiration for my teacher doubled.

Looks as if I was destined to be a grammarian after passing through an apprenticeship in literature with our class teacher, Shri D K Kulkarni, in the last two years of high school, the tenth and eleventh years in those days. He taught us English, literary selections, grammar, and composition. He used to encourage us to put questions about whatever he happened to be teaching. The pleasure he took in this activity was so obvious that the last quarter of the school hour often turned into a discussion session. At one point I asked him about some detail of English grammar that puzzled me. Instead of lucidly explaining that point as he usually did, he suggested that I look him up later in the teacher's common room so that we could talk about it. So, when I saw him in the school recess I was naturally in some trepidation, wondering what faux pas I had committed. He quietly led me by the hand to the adjoining school library hall, stopped at a shelf marked 'Grammar' and took out a couple of volumes, *The Philosophy of Grammar* and

Language: Its Nature, Development and Origin, both by the renowned Danish scholar, Otto Jespersen. Putting these into my hands and suggesting that in future I take up my puzzlements with 'this fine gentleman'. Wittingly or unwittingly, a kindly school teacher had introduced me to a torchbearer, who made sure that I later found early American Linguistic structuralism not wholly satisfying.

Now comes my apprenticeship in English literature as an undergraduate. Two of my teachers, Shri M G Bhate (who combined an MA in English with a London School BSc in Economics) and Shri G P Pradhan (who combined an infectious zest for literature with a jail term in India's freedom struggle in the past and a jail term during free India's Emergency in his future). Shri Bhate introduced me to the importance of the *scrutiny* critics and the socio-economic background of literature, and Shri Pradhan to the sheer enjoyment of literature and placing it in the context of life. In their differing ways, both had the ability to get even the backbenchers in the class excited and to inculcate a love of Shakespeare. (In later life, when it was suggested to me that a patriotic Indian couldn't possibly love English literature or that a socially committed reader of literature ought not possibly indulge in the frivolity of enjoying literary beauty I was, and still am, all incomprehension.)

And finally, my experience of doing a doctorate in an American university, a far western outpost of European civilization. I duly drafted my doctoral thesis on Marathi phonology and morphology and handed in the draft to my research supervisor, Professor Charles Hockett at Cornell University. He said he'll go through it and I should report to him in a week's time. Having heard blood-curdling stories about the doings of Professor Hockett's red-ink pen, I was in some trepidation when he later handed my draft back to me totally unscathed. I was wondering to myself whether he found it too unworthy even to touch with his red-ink pen, when he broke in : "You could give it to the typist, no problem. Well, actually there are four spots wherein you have in passing raised problems about some of my views on points of linguistic analysis. In two cases you have succeeded in convincing me of my error and in the other two you haven't but really you have argued your point well, which is all that matters in a doctoral thesis." I was taken aback, unable to imagine an Indian research supervisor doing anything of the kind. Having recovered from the shock, I realized that I had duly earned the right to call him Charles rather than Professor Hockett as I had been doing so far. I was inoculated against the colonial hangover for life.

Later, when I found myself in the shoes of a teacher, I wondered from time to time how I fared as a teacher in the eyes of my students. Quite a few of them told me after we got to know each other better. They told me about their puzzlement about me. In sum, their puzzlement was as to whether I was a starlet taskmaster or an indulgent senior friend, for I was both by turns. They couldn't place me; they couldn't because they had no pigeonhole for the fusion mode, being good Indians. Mine was a fusion mode in quite another sense too. I was doing a stint as a visiting professor in a university language and literature department, lecturing on linguistic and literary theory by turns. It was a composite group of those doing their respective MA in English and Marathi. Once I sought to draw a student out informally on how my use of English worked on the classroom floor. He assured me that there was no problem even with students of Marathi (as he was). As he warmed to the subject, he casually remarked about my fusion mode: "You have truly introduced us to the linguistic and literary thinkers; it is as if the other day we were listening to a round-table debate on poetic theory that was going on with Aristotle and Abhinavagupta, Jnane svara and Coleridge, Richards and D K Bedekar participating." It was a humbling experience for me to realize that I had unwittingly afforded my students such a globalizing learning experience and in part repaid my debt (*rna*) to my teachers.

Perhaps, my two fusion modes, the *guru-pupil* and *acharya-student* mode on the one hand and the mode exploiting the double intellectual inheritance, Indian and European on the other hand, are not two distinct fusion modes at all but a single composite Indian-European globalizing teaching mode after all.

Part II

College and University Teachers

> What the teacher is,
> is more important than
> what he teaches.
>
> – *Karl Menninger*

A Prayer for Talib

Amrik Singh

Two very different teachers of mine from my schools days come to my mind readily. The first I remember easily because he used to hit me for eating nuts in class. I had a friend who was addicted to this habit and I too had picked it up. My teacher did not approve of this habit and would punish both of us off and on.

I also remember another teacher from my secondary level days for a different reason. He tried to encourage me to improve my performance in the class. That was the phase in my life when I was more interested in general reading than in classroom assignments. This habit has stayed with me all my life. In a sense, I am glad that I did not come under the influence of this particular teacher. The habit of general reading which I acquired during those days has given me both knowledge and the joy of knowledge. But for this asset, my life would have been somewhat dull. Fortunately, both these teachers made no impression on me.

However, it was in college, and that too during the second year, that I came into contact with the teacher who had a life-long impact on me. His name was Gurbachan Singh Talib. *Talib* is a Persian word, which means a supplicant. Although he did not write poetry, he used this *nom de plume.* Hardly anyone referred to him by his first name. It was always the nom de plume which was used.

During those days, college education was spread over two stages; it was 2+2, to use the current parlance. In the second year of my college, I unexpectedly won a prize for standing second in English in class. The custom was to give books by way of a prize. This particular teacher was in charge of that activity. I went up to him and asked him to give me a book which I would find interesting. He selected a book by Theodre Dresier, a novel entitled *An American Tragedy* for me. It was a long novel and it took me three days of nonstop reading to finish it. I remember lots of details of this novel even now and have also read various other novels by the same novelist.

It was this incidental development which brought me into contact with him. In the third year, I drew closer to him. I started visiting him at home and there were many long conversations. Each one of them gave me a feeling of getting enriched as well as stimulated in the right sense of the word. He would guide me in my reading and help me in a variety of ways. I did exceedingly well in history and was inclined to take up a Master's course in that subject. But he was a teacher of English and I too had some interest in it. Largely under his influence therefore, I opted for a Master's course in English. In the course of those two years, he also loaned me many of his books.

It was when I passed out and got appointed as a teacher that I faced a problem. There was nobody around to instruct me on how to lecture. Before I went to meet the first batch of students, I had to make up my mind as to how I would go about the job. One easy option was to follow the style of teaching practiced by another teacher of mine, a Bengali gentleman. He had gone to Oxford in 1938 but had come home to be with the family at the end of one year. Meanwhile the war broke out and he could not go back till after the war. During this interval, he got a job in the college at Amritsar where I was studying.

He was an excellent teacher. His main strength lay in the fact that he had everything worked out in advance by way of points and could take them up one by one and expound the details in their proper sequence. There was seldom an overlap in what he said. More than that, he was always precise and to the point. These things attracted me to him.

I started following that method only to discover that I was not as systematic as he was, with the result that, after a few days I began to lose my bearings. It was in that situation that I thought of my other teacher, G S Talib. His mode of teaching was to take up a topic, talk about it and build up his argument and build it up so well, that at the end of the class, one felt sated with what the teacher had set out to explain.

His technique in brief, was to have a clear focus on the theme, and then build around it step by step; not always following a pre-worked arrangement yet sustaining the logic of his argument. Sometimes he would go forwards and sometimes backwards but he never lost the main thrust of the argument. Eventually, it was this technique which I thought suited my own way of thinking.

A few weeks later, when I had my first meeting with him after I became a teacher, he asked me probing questions as to what kind of technique I had developed for myself. In a bumbling sort of way, I described to him what I had been doing. He smiled and said, "Everyone has to develop his own technique."

A couple of months later, I discovered for myself that, though I got a lot of satisfaction from following my teacher's style of teaching, it required drastic amendment. I discovered for myself that while the more intelligent students reacted favorably to this style of lecturing, it went above the head of a large number of the other students. This was quite disconcerting. Thereupon I modified my style once again.

In the course of my long teaching career, I have discovered one simple fact: unless one repeats what one has said and repeats it in a different way every time, the average student does not entirely follow what the teacher is trying to say. If one repeats, more than half the students get involved in what one is teaching. This means that something like two thirds of the students react favorably to what is being said in the classroom. The remaining one third are unable to respond unless they are given extra attention. The only way to ensure that they too respond is to find the time to repeat yet again. Some times it was possible to do that but more often it was not. So this was the technique I evolved for myself, inspired by my teacher's words.

As I grew in the profession, Talib and I became close friends. Our friendship continued till the very end. He passed away some years ago after a long and eventful career. He wrote more than a dozen books and translated the *Adi Granth* into English. This was quite an achievement and he is widely remembered for it.

Electricity at First Sight
V V Athani

Professor R S Tilwalli was Assistant Professor of Electrical Engineering when I joined the Department of Electrical Engineering in the Government College of Engineering, Pune as a student. He taught us Electrical Machines and Electrical Measurements. I vividly remember his use of the Fleming's left hand rule for motor action and Fleming's right hand rule for generator action. Whenever we nodded our heads to a teacher's familiar question: "Have you understood?", he used to say that when he had been studying and teaching induction motors for thirty years, and still could not say for sure that he had understood the motor, how could we claim to have understood it after listening to one lecture of his? He made us pour over half a dozen books on electric motors and acquire proficiency in the subject. My habit of acquiring proficiency in whatever subject I studied and taught is due to Professor Tilwalli.

When he shifted later to Walchand College of Engineering, Sangli as Professor and Head, Electrical Engineering Department, he called on me to serve as the subject expert in the Board of Studies of Shivaji University to which his college was affiliated. I felt honoured and complied, no questions asked.

The second teacher who influenced me profoundly was Professor Venkata Rao. He was my Professor at the Indian

Institute of Science, Bangalore where I did my ME in Power Engineering. His subject was Control Systems. He used to teach it with such exuberance and energy that we could not help getting infected by his enthusiasm. By the time his lecture came to an end, he used to get so exhausted that he used to lightly ask us, panting for breath at the same time: "Have I succeeded in thoroughly confusing you?" and we would sing in a chorus: "Yes, sir." Professor Rao was the teacher who was responsible for creating in me an abiding interest in Control Systems.

My third great mentor has been Professor M E Van Valkenberg, a world-renowned authority on Electric Circuits and Networks as well as Systems. I consider myself very fortunate that I had the opportunity of taking the Network Synthesis course offered by him at the University of Illinois at Urbana-Champaign (UIUC) where I did my MS degree programme. When I first saw him in the class, a feeling of such reverence welled up in my heart that the following line from the Bhagavad-Gita came to my lips: "Tad viddhi pranipaaten pariprashnena sevayaa" (Acquire that knowledge by prostrating in reverence, by asking questions during discussions, and by serving your Guru.)

He was such a gifted teacher that every time I had a discussion with him, I felt he had graced me. My decision to specialize in Control Systems was due to the inspiration he had provided me.

A Future in the Past

Sushma Varma

Most people regard history as an outdated subject, but I regard history as the Prince of all subjects. Without history you cannot study any subject.

I still remember the day when I told my father, a scientist that I wanted to specialise in history. His immediate reaction was, "Study history but learn to live in the future and not the past." I realised later that it was he who had understood the importance of history.

While my father encouraged me to study history it was my teacher, Professor A R Kulkarni, the renowned historian of Maratha history who taught me how to research history.

I had to write a term paper for my MA course. The topic was "Source Material Available for Writing Maratha History". My friend went to the library and borrowed all the books on her card and on mine. After she finished her assignment, she avoided giving me the books, on some pretext or the other. On the given day, just before beginning his class Professor Kulkarni said, "First give me your term papers." That day, as ill luck would have it, I happened to be sitting right in front of him. He lost his temper with me and with all those who had not completed their assignments. He uttered some really harsh words, which upset me a lot because for the first time in my student life, I had been scolded by a teacher. After the lecture, I went straight to my friend's hostel, borrowed the library books from her and went home. I started going through them but found nothing constructive; so I took out the class notes, wrote the term paper and submitted it the next day.

Professor Kulkarni, I think, was very anxious to know his students and did his homework quite fast. Next week he came to the class with the corrected term papers. I still remember we used to write in long sized notebooks. Mine was yellow in color; it was kept right down. The thought of his reaction really made me shiver. As he returned the term papers he went on explaining the writer's mistakes. When my turn came, he said, "This assignment is the best. It shows a lot of research aptitude." I was amazed because at that time I did not even know that one could research in history. I had thought one could research only in science. On the last day of the academic year, after the farewell party he told me, "After the results are out, come and see me, I want you to research on Mountstuart Elphinstone." I had never heard this name before.

After the results were out I was not happy with my marks. I was returning home, crestfallen. He saw me and sent the peon to call me. He called me to the department and spoke to me. He explained to me that it is difficult to get a first class in history and that he was quite satisfied with my marks. He sent the peon to buy a PhD application form for me and showed me how to fill it. After filling the form, I told him that I would do a PhD only if I get a scholarship. He only said, "I will see. First get registered." I did succeed in getting the scholarship and thus started my journey into research.

While researching I found it very difficult to work on Mountstuart Elphinestone as two top historians had already written extensively on him. I was rather nervous. Every time I went to Professor Kulkarni he would say, "When you work in the archives you will understand your topic." After going through all the published work, I started working in the Peshwa Daftar, Pune. For one year I read from 10.30 am to 4.00 pm. If I had any difficulty in deciphering a document, my guide would always find the time to help me out even though he was very busy since he held a number of positions.

While going through the documents I began to understand the complex reality of the time when the document was written. I came across the same documents, which had been used by the two historians earlier and saw how they used only that part which proved their viewpoint. It was then that I understood how one must challenge an existing research work. I now realized why my guide kept telling me "Go to the archives." He always insisted on the study of original sources and he would never sign a PhD thesis until a student had read and used original sources. I visited the Maharashtra State Archives, Mumbai and the National Archives, New Delhi. I had consulted all the material available in India. Only the material available in India Office, London remained unvisited. As luck would have it, my guide had to go to London for his research. He brought for me the documents that I needed. Actually in his absence I had finished writing my final draft but after getting the new material, I had to rewrite it as the entire format of my thesis had changed, to incorporate the new prospective. This meant another six months of work but then it was worth it because it had added credibility and authenticity to my work.

The day I submitted my PhD thesis he informed me that there was a lecturer's post in the department and that I should apply for the sake of experience. After the interview he told me frankly that he had not recommended me as he felt I was too young to teach postgraduate students. He was overruled and I got the job. Despite his reservations he welcomed me as his 'juniormost colleague'. I think I learnt as much from him in the five years that I spent as his colleague as I did as his student.

A Scroll of Honour

P C Shejwalkar

All along I have been very fortunate in getting benevolent teachers in school, in college, as well as when I undertook doctoral and research work. I am permanently indebted to all these teachers, who always gave me an insight into my own personality. Among all these teachers, there was one whose leadership and humanitarian outlook, has meant the most in my life. He was the learned professor of Economics, Dr T M Joshi, who was then the principal of the well-known Brihan Maharashtra College of Commerce (BMCC). His entire personality epitomized compassion as well as creativity. He always placed before me a set of values, which would enable me to complete my doctoral studies.

I registered as a PhD student with Dr Joshi as my Research Guide somewhere in 1955 and I found that right from the first day, he had started taking a keen interest in my work. Though he was busy as the principal of the College, and with duties at the University, he always made it a point to give me special time. He used to be free for a while in the evening before dinner, so he would ask me to come over with my notes and would listen to me reading out what I had written. I have hardly seen any research guides who spend their evenings on reading theses and giving their students thoughtful guidance. However Dr Joshi would do just that. He would suggest novel alternatives in my statements and I would add them to my research work. His knowledge was perfect and up-to-date, and his command over English was impeccable.

It was not just for his knowledge and his sense of involvement in my work that I was impressed but also for his most compassionate and sentimental relationship with me that changed my mindset and made me into an extremely confident person. Even after my research work was over, he continued to act as my mentor. As my friend, philosopher and guide, he took pains to do everything possible to enlighten me with new facts and new perspectives, and thus to direct my career the right way. He proposed my name in the Deccan Education Society – as a Life Member – where he acts as a trustee in the management. He continued to be my guide even after that since I really needed someone to advise me as to how I should handle people such as my subordinates and students.

He was a role-model for me in my relationship with my students. He had set a shining example before me to help poor and needy students. During my career of over 40 years as a teacher and administrator, I have seen to it that any student who comes to me with a problem must go back with a smiling face. I have been able to do this because of the art of developing relationships which I had learnt from my mentor, Dr Joshi. It was because of his blessings that I was able to get important positions in the university as well as in public life. It was he who advised me to apply for a capsule course of four months in management offered by the Indian Institute of Management, Calcutta. Studying management gave another beautiful turn to my life. It was because of this qualification that I could introduce full-time MBA programmes in Pune well before many others. Dr Joshi settled down in the USA after 1965. He used to always write back to me promptly whenever I wanted his guidance.

Whatever I am today is indeed because of him. His code of conduct, his warmth, his smiling face, his pursuit of knowledge, and his excellence in teaching Advanced Economics had a tremendous impact on me during my student years. I still do not know how to repay this debt to him. The only thing that I do know is that he is no more. I often look at his portrait kept in my house and observe the Dr T M Joshi Memorial Day in my management institute every 24th February. I also meticulously follow the advice he gave me from time to time. If there is some such thing as rebirth, I would always pray to God that I get Dr Joshi as my mentor in every life.

The Mathematical Comic

Roop Karnani

The transition from school to college is on the one hand a transition from a disciplined life to a lot of freedom, and on the other, from studying subjects from a single text-book to referring multiple, thick textbooks. Maths, which appeared to be simple in school, suddenly became complicated with trigonometry, calculus, matrices, and a host of other topics. Even today, for students opting for the science stream, maths is one of the most difficult subjects. But ...

Way back in the 1970s, the students of Wadia College, Pune were blessed with a comical genius called Professor Hoshang D Moogat. He did not believe in theoretical knowledge but on the very first day of college he put everybody at ease by solving simple problems which had already appeared in the university exams, making maths look so easy. He also had a knack of interspersing the lectures with anecdotes and a lot of fun and entertainment, making even dry and boring calculations very enjoyable. His anecdotes were such that every one of the students could identify himself with his narratives. This made him the 'darling' not only of the students of Wadia college, but also from other colleges — since many non-Wadians too would flock to his classes, like people come to a cinema. The hall which could accommodate 120 Wadians, would be packed with over

200 students, obviously 80 of them outsiders. There would be no place to sit in the classroom; so the students stood on all sides of the hall, and listened to his lectures.

It is common knowledge that a maths problem can be solved in more ways than one. But other professors would insist on only teaching the textbook methods, which were lengthy and complicated. Moogat possessed a knack, as if a magical wand, for solving a problem in just a few simple methods and mathematically correct steps. Not only would he do this himself, but he would also encourage students to think on their own and find shorter methods.

Very often, an ordinary student would stand up while Moogat was solving a problem on the blackboard, and suggest a different step from Moogat's. Moogat would quickly anticipate that the student had a shorter method than his. Immediately he would order everyone to listen to the student in respectful silence. He would then encourage him to dictate the steps and, without any ego hassles, praise him in front of the whole class for giving him the new method. His genuine appreciation of the student's innovative thinking encouraged all the students to make an effort and come out with new methods.

But at the same time his motto was 'practice makes a man perfect' and he would grill the students by making them solve a large number of problems. Usually his was the last lecture of the day and the longest. Whatever he wrote on the board, he insisted that the students too write it, along with him. No homework, no solving problems at home — everything had to be done along with him in class. I remember we used to fill ten notebooks of 400 pages each, through the year, with Moogat's notes and solved problems. Yet we never felt bored of attending his class. Maths was fun when Moogat taught it.

During revision before the exams, we referred to all of the 4,000 pages, and never found it tedious or time-consuming.

Because, as Moogat would put it, he had 'dinned' it into our 'nuts'. Many ordinary students like me did not even need to study for the paper, because he had attuned us to solve all the difficult problems expected in the university and IIT entrance exams. We knew his line of thinking and would adapt just that. He had made maths wizards out of us.

I recall that many of the short methods that I had suggested were taught to his subsequent batches. He would call them 'Roop's method'. And like that for all such students. Many of his students became top scholars in maths, and made a mark in the best universities around the world — MIT, Caltech and the IITs.

He used to often quote an example of one of his students called Chaudhary. Chaudhary used to solve 12 questions in an exam paper, where he had a choice of attempting just eight, and he would request the examiner to correct any eight because he was confident that all his problems had been solved correctly. He used to tell us that Chaudhary's answer papers are preserved in the Poona University for posterity. Moogat would tell us that the proofs of well-known theorems enunciated by great mathematicians were resolved in an innovative way by some of his students in much shorter ways. What's more, even foreign authors had acknowledged and incorporated these methods into their textbooks. These stories of ordinary Indian students becoming heroes would encourage us to use our brains rather than blindly follow textbooks. And this habit of independent thinking has helped us throughout our lives.

Moogat's antics in the class would keep the students in excellent humor. He used to often repeat the formulae in a musical singsong tone and even dance to his own tune, making the class sing with him. We never forgot the formulae.

He was a good counselor and patiently listened to his students' personal problems. He was our friend, philosopher and guide. Even when he gave tuitions to students, he never bothered to ask for the fee. He knew that some of the students were financially weak. So he would never embarrass them by asking for his fee, yet he would teach them with the same vigor.

Today, his students have reached astronomical positions and are spread all over the world. But none can forget him. If today they meet him, he may not remember them; but to them he is still their 'darling' professor. I too am still in awe of him and this is my small tribute to a living maths genius and wonderful human being!

A Legacy Unforgotten

Rehana Ghadially

In shaping personality and character, the family takes the primary place. However, educational institutions such as school and college are powerful tools in molding our behavior and setting some of our priorities. As a young woman in college my family, teachers and peers jostled for priority in shaping me. My mother chiseled me in what constitutes a 'good girl', imprinting on me the importance of grinding *masala* on a stone, getting the *chappati* roasted just right on the hot *tava* and changing the living room curtains. During vacation, my father gave me work from our shop and taught me the importance of hard work and value of money. Classmates at college pulled me into the world of ease and leisure — hanging around the canteen and eyeing the boys, bunking class and going to the movies, eating *dosa* and chatting at the nearby Udipi joint. Simultaneously, they emphasized the value of getting a good class and percentage in the exams.

My teachers at St Xavier's College on the other hand expected high academic standards from us. In the confusion of these contradictory demands, one person stood out above all others as my role model. This was my teacher — Father James Fillela at St Xavier's College — a Jesuit priest from Spain who taught me Psychology.

Young, thin, tall, handsome with sparkling eyes behind plain black-rimmed glasses he exuded confidence and struck an authoritative yet benign pose. A perennial grin on his face seemed to mock at our immaturity and helplessness and kept all forty-eight young women enrolled in the Psychology program enthralled. As young women coping with our budding biology we were bonded with our teacher by a chemical equation and an inexplicable crush on him The two male students (one of them was a priest anyway) in our class and other male students on the campus did not seem to matter as much. This attraction contributed to our drive to please him, and what pleased him most was academics.

Students at Xavier's were not simply biological entities, they were women with substance and intellect. They were attracted not just by his youthful physique but also by his qualities as a teacher and general personality as well. He came to class on time with well-prepared notes and never missed a class. These are the minimum requirements of a fine teacher.

With his mastery over the English language and a commanding style of communication, he nourished our interest in human behavior. By his own example he set a tone in class to demand more from ourselves and strive for academic excellence. This was evident when his grin turned into a soft smile as he saw his students sitting in the library or on the library steps and studying. He was thrilled when we did well in the Board exams. When I stood first in Bombay University in the Psychology section he said, "You were a clear case for a first class, the other two were given a slight push." These words were heaven to my ears and I could see the pride on his face.

Father was kind, straightforward and fair, yet favored those who excelled in scholarly pursuits. He maintained the right amount of distance, not too far as to be unapproachable and not so near as to lose some of the mystique. A pious figure, he demonstrated to us the possibility of combining that which is the best in matters of the mind and the spirit.

After getting my Bachelor's degree program, I decided to go to the United States for further studies. He wrote me a letter of recommendation for entrance into the postgraduate program there, a copy of it I preserved for a long time. My brother was the engine behind my wish to study abroad but the guiding spirit was my Jesuit teacher at college. I too wanted a doctoral degree like him and to teach Psychology.

On completion of my postgraduate studies in the United States and having landed a job in a premium institute in India, shortly after my return, I invited my teacher home for lunch. We sat chatting for some time and then as Father took a short nap, I wondered if I had at last fulfilled my fantasy and the dream of all my college classmates. I kept in touch with my teacher of and on. He retired and left for Spain and kept in touch for a while. Now I get only silence from my e-mail sent to him.

What is the legacy of Father James Fillela and my other Jesuit teachers at college? I would say it is the aura they created — a love for learning, a safe, gentle, clean atmosphere, the importance of simple pleasures as sources of happiness. In short, a balance between play, piety and scholarship. Could a young person have asked for more? Could this be the reason that material pursuits have never given me joy and satisfaction? I often wonder.

The Physics of Humanity

Subroto Roy

When I was pursuing my first year of BSc Physics, I had a special dislike for a teacher of thermodynamics as she appeared rigid and rather poor in her spoken English. You know when students with an English medium school background encounter anyone with a vernacular background they tend to look down upon her or him saying, "God only knows how this person has passed their MSc; he or she doesn't even know English!"

I was no exception to this attitude but somewhere at the back of my mind there was a lot of respect for the 'Teacher'. However, when I attended this teacher's lectures it was more often than not a dimming experience. I would obviously want to find fault with her.

I found a suitable opportunity one day to prove to my classmates that the teacher was not very good. While teaching thermodynamics, this teacher said in the passing that an x quantity (considerable at that) of heat would be wasted in a certain process. I immediately jumped onto my toes to tell her my views on this in an attempt to refute her. I said, "The heat energy is not wasted." She was intrigued and said, "Tell me how you can use this heat energy." I did not hesitate to say that this heat could be used in a thermocouple situation to produce electricity. She was dumbfounded but not offended! As she was a person with an open and fair mind (which I came to know later), she told me to make an electronic diagram so as to incorporate this thermocouple and try to show that this heat can practically be used.

She continued as my Physics teacher in my second year too. But as luck would have it, I scored badly in the second year. I was very downcast. At that time, it was this teacher (she was known as Mrs Gupta) who came up to me and asked in her incorrect English, "Subroto, you are so clever. Why you can't score well in exams? Do you need any help?"

Those words of concern and acknowledgement of my intellect made up for my poor performance. The lesson I learnt was to give top priority to humaneness and not so much to erudition, expertise, intellect or any capability that does not heed understanding humanity.

Nobel Teacher

A N Maheshwari

My association with Professor Chandrasekhar dates back to 1964 when I joined the University of Chicago to do my PhD in Physics. I saw an Indian looking professor dressed in a black suit and a Cambridge University tie sitting in the first row of a Physics colloquium and could make out that the distinguished person was Professor Chandrasekhar, whom everybody affectionately called Chandra. He appeared to me then both very reserved and unapproachable. I changed this opinion as I began to know him more closely. My next encounter with Chandra was at a Phi-Club meeting, which was specially arranged by the Department of Physics of the University to provide face-to-face interactions to the fresh class of graduate students with the senior faculty of the University. Professor Chandrasekhar spoke on the General Theory of Relativity and its relevance to Cosmology and Astrophysics. I do not think I followed the lecture but can distinctly recall the remark made by Chandra: "Veracity of Einstein's theory of Gravitation is as undisputed as the findings of Justice Warren on the assassination of President John F Kennedy". I left the meeting with more awe and a feeling of a vast distance between his intellectual abilities and what I possessed as a twenty-one year old graduate student. I was thrilled to see the announcement that Professor

Chandrasekhar would teach a course on Non-relativistic quantum mechanics as a part of the MSc course in Physics at the University of Delhi. I signed up for it perhaps thinking that I should be able to impress the professor with my background and the head start I thought I had. In the first lecture the professor entered the room and demanded that the 'No Smoking' rule be observed, as he was allergic to tobacco smoke. This was obeyed by the class but Chandra's reasons were suspect as he would often be seen sitting between Professor Mark Ingraham and Professor Gregor Wentzel both of whom puffed away at their cigars continuously and within their vicinity the pollution level could only be matched by coal-fed boilers in Chicago City.

Chandra spoke Cambridge-English without a trace of American accent and wrote on the blackboard as though he was doing calligraphy. He did not like being disturbed during his lecture and looked reprovingly at students drinking coffee or eating sandwiches. The course was uneventful as it progressed but a jolt was experienced by the entire class when he announced at the end of the eleventh week that the examination would be of six hours' duration with an optimum response time of about four hours. He further elaborated that there would be only one problem to be solved in closed-book/closed-notes setting and that rough-calculation sheets were to be appended to the answer-script. He also advised students to bring their packed lunch to the examination hall. The problems to be solved turned out to be on finding analytically changes in energy levels of hydrogen atom in strong electric field by setting up the Hamiltonian and writing the Schrodinger equation. Hints were given for various stages of the solution that could be reached after about each successive hour of work. I vaguely recall that I could not proceed further beyond the fourth hour and closed my test after eating sandwiches, which I had specially prepared and rounded up my snack with an apple. I wrote from National Radio Astronomy Observatory, Green Bank, where I had gone to undergo summer training, with misgivings, to the Graduate Students Advisor of the Department of Physics to let me know how I had fared in Professor Chandrasekhar's course and whether the University would continue to give me financial assistance in the next academic year. I received a reassuring reply that Professor Chandrasekhar was happy with my performance and that the University would be pleased to support my further graduate studies. I have narrated this incident at length because it brings out how deep a teacher probed the mind of each of his students, painstakingly and without complaining of the inordinate demand on his time in spite of his own pressures of research and other professional commitments. Although, I chose to work in the field of theoretical high-energy Physics, not the direct research interest of Professor Chandrasekhar, Chandra decided to be one of the four advisors who supervised my doctoral studies. I began to experience Chandra's warmth from the smile on his face in acknowledging my greetings. Gradually I started to know the real Chandra and Mrs Chandrasekhar. Occasionally I would join both of them at dinner table in the restaurant of the International House and listen to episodes from the life of the esteemed professor as narrated by his wife. She knew how uncomfortable students were in Chandra's presence. I felt elated and inspired on being chosen to share stories from the life of the great man.

I would like to contribute to this essay one story on how Chandra handled his graduate students, because I was the second party in the incident. I wanted to fix up with my advisory group the date and time for holding an assessment, a requirement of the PhD course. Meeting Chandra in his office in the Laboratory for Space Research and Astrophysics was difficult as an appointment was required. I knew Chandra's daily habits and decided to catch him during his walk to the laboratory. I accosted Chandra and asked point blank whether he would be in station on such and such date and whether he could be available for conducting my assessment. He suggested that I defer the assessment for a week. I told him, "Chandra, do I not come under your priority and can you not spare half-an-hour for a graduate student?" Chandra's immediate response was a 'yes' to the scheduling of my assessment on the date I had proposed but he said," Maheshwari, can you explain the concept of negative temperature?" Chandra continued to remind me whenever I met him and since then I had pleaded with him to postpone the assessment for another month so I could prepare myself better. In between I used to meet Chandra to discuss Physics and sometimes he would walk to me at my desk with some newspaper report on India in his hand and share his anguish. He once asked me to explain to him the concept of pseudo energy-momentum tensor for the gravitational field. I felt honoured in having been approached by the professor and specially privileged when Professor Chandrasekhar gave me a person-to-person seminar on how he had used this concept in his research work. This aspect of his life is also important because *he took pride in pointing out that he benefited in research more from his students than from his colleagues* in the University. In 1969 he told me that during the course of his career in the University except for one research paper, which he had jointly written with Enrico Fermi, all his research work was either independent or was carried out with his graduate students.

He would emphasize to me the importance of diligence and observance of discipline in daily working habits. He emphasized that personal targets be continually advanced so that life may remain an unending challenge without ever getting the feeling of having arrived at. He once mentioned that in having decided to live abroad he could only live the life of a scientist. From his own experience he pointed out that the life of a scientist in a foreign country is extremely difficult and very rarely, and only very few people, can hope to contribute to science at levels that bring lasting recognition and scientific immortality. At the age of nineteen, Chandrasekhar had made the scientific discovery of the existence of a fundamental stellar mass from his study of the Physics of white dwarf stars, the famous Chandrasekhar limit. Although Chandrasekhar had carried out his monumental work during his long sea voyage to England from India in 1930 and published it in 1931 in the Astrophysical Journal of the University of Chicago, he was awarded the Nobel Prize in Physics for this work only in 1983.

Chandra did not let recognition slow down his pace of work and kept on moving his targets throughout his life; to wit Physics of white dwarf, stellar structures and radiative transfer, magneto-hydrodynamics, mathematical theory of black holes, the study of Newton's Principia.

He was a perfect embodiment of what he practiced and his advice to his students was based on his experience. He might have influenced me in deciding to return to India after getting my PhD degree. In what follows next I would describe the role he played in my later professional life.

Professor Chandrasekhar was happy to know when I informed him that I had joined the university at Simla. Once, he wrote to me that while taking a walk at Aspen in the Rocky Mountains in the USA he imagined that in Simla I would also be similarly situated in an ideal setting, conducive for pursuing theoretical Physics. Soon after, in early 1973 I met Chandra in New Delhi. He asked me how I was progressing and if there was something he could do to help me. I told Chandra, "Nice climate and beautiful natural environment are fine but I need journals to do my scientific work, which the new University I had joined was unable to provide me." Chandra instantaneously decided to gift to the Himachal Pradesh university his personal collection of journals. Within three months of that fateful meeting the Himachal Pradesh University received collections dating back to 1935 of *The Physical Review*, *The Physical Review Letters* and *The Reviews of Modern Physics*. This gift by Professor Chandrasekhar was without any expectation for return except that the journals should be made available for research consultation to all students and faculty.

This act of generosity is unparalleled and brings out his genuine concern for his students and interest in their academic growth.

What has been described here is a humble tribute of an Eklavya to his Dronacharya. His other pupils will have similar stories to recount of how this great teacher influenced their lives.

Great and Godly

Kumarendra Mallick

A long journey along the narrow streak of time came to a pause on December 31, 2001. On this day I laid down my office with a fair measure of satisfaction. On this occasion I was asked to say a few words. While walking up to the dais I tried to look back in the years. The self-reflecting milestones at different points of time, not equidistant though, flashed by one-by-one. I clearly recalled that Thursday morning when my mother fed me *kheer* (rice cooked in sweetened milk) and my father carried me on his shoulders to get me admitted to our village school. I had a slate of medium size and a few chalk pieces in a small box. The starting of a journey…

Shri Vishnu Sethi, my first teacher, took me in his arms and made me sit on the ground next to him. Most of the children were from our neighbourhood and I did not feel the difference between home and school (except that now we couldn't climb the mango tree that grew in our backyard). After making me comfortable, Vishnu Sir drew three perfect circles on my slate. I traced the circles again and again, and again for about four hours every day and for ten full days uttering Brahma, Vishnu and Maheshwar – three circles and three gods standing for creation (of good qualities), sustenance (of higher nature) and destruction (of negative attributes). Vishnu Sir appears and reappears at the back of my mind whenever somebody appreciates my handwriting that was set while tracing the perfect circles or whenever I recite or hear somebody else, reciting, "Guru Brahma, Guru Vishnu, Gurudev Maheshwar . . ."

After my early education in the village school, I moved to Cuttack, a historic town and capital of the then Orissa in 1954. On Wednesday the 6th August, I joined the famous Ravenshaw Collegiate School. The majestic building of the Orissa High Court is situated in front of the school main gate.

The School was established in 1829 by T E Ravenshaw, a great educationist and the then Commissioner of Orissa, had during the first hundred years of its history, the distinction of having their students top the matriculation examination 70 times among four states – Bengal, Bihar, Orissa and Assam! Famous leaders like Netaji Subhash Chandra Bose, Madhusudan Das, Bijju Patnaik, Nabakrushna Choudhury, Radhanath Rath, scientists like Dr P K Parija, Professor Jogesh Pati, historian R C Mazumdar, the swimmer Mihir Sen, the first Indian to cross the British Channel, many academicians, jurists, writers, poets, sports persons and freedom fighters once played hide and seek in the corridors of this school with a sprawling campus.

Father-like teachers, Sri Narayan Pati, Sri Niranjan Mohapatra, Sri B Narayana Murthy, Sri Kailash Chandra Roy and many more were role models. My overall development took shape here. I cannot understand how these teachers could devote so much time to us in the classroom, in the hostel, in the playground, in yoga classes, in carrying out social work and in organizing school functions. My chest swells up when I think that we were no less than their own offsprings.

Sri Niranjan Mohapatra, the most popular teacher in the entire town of Cuttack was known for his kindness, excellent teaching, concern for the student community and for his love for sports. He always wished me to top the state matriculation examination. About a month before the final examination he took a preparatory class test in history. A classmate of mine forgot to bring his notebook. He borrowed mine and wrote the answers. He did not put down his name through oversight. I answered the questions in another notebook. Niranjan Sir happened to first pick up my friend's answer book to evaluate. Seeing my name on the notebook and the marks scored, he was crestfallen! He wrote the answers himself in the same notebook and assigned the marks he expected me to score. After going through several answer books, suddenly he discovered another answer book carrying my name. He quickly evaluated it and put the same marks he had given a few hours back to his own answers. Immediately I was summoned and my left ear was screwed more to express his concealed relief at my preparedness for the examination than as punishment for exchanging the notebook.

Looking back and recalling this incident I cannot measure the fullness of Niranjan Sir's concern and love for his students! Till today I feel sorry for him and cannot forgive myself that I did not top the matriculation examination in 1958; a poor consolation that I was a distant eighth in the state merit list. Had I scored just nine marks more, I would have got the second rank! But "a narrow miss, is as good as a mile" as the adage goes.

When I think of Ravenshaw Collegiate School any time now, those beautiful days in the classroom with my classmates – Gitimoy Kar who later on moved to USA and worked in the development of fibre optics with Corning, footballers Gopal Pal and Kabuli, Samar Ballav Mohapatra, Secretary to the Government of India and many more – and the football matches in the torrential Cuttack rains in the famous Sunshine ground on the banks of the river Kathjori, readily come crowding to my mind.

In 1958, I joined Ravenshaw College. Although my stay for intermediate studies was just two years, I came into contact with some brilliant teachers – Professor Dayanidhi Pattnaik, who later joined the Bhoodan movement, Professor Sri Ramchandra Das who kept the entire college spellbound with his scholarly lectures, Professors Brundaban Acharya, Pranabandhu Kar, Gokulan and Mohapatra and Kulamani Samal – all excellent teachers and excellent human beings. Till this day, whenever I step into the college, the hostel, where I lived or the college library, I get a thrill and my eyes search for the sands on which we had once moved.

The doors to a new world opened up when I entered IIT Kharagpur in July 1960. The sprawling campus, the imposing institute building, well-designed hostels named after statesmen, well-meaning seniors eager to interface with the newcomers with a cementing stuff called ragging – by and large enjoyable in the 1960s – god-like loving teachers, excellent teaching and all other facilities starting from sports, music, photography, entertainment, literary activities to romance. Plenty of everything: plenty of fun, plenty of hard work, plenty of leisure and plenty of marks, too.

On my first day in the department, our Head, Professor T C Bagchi, put his hand on my shoulder and said, "Kumarendra, you are from Ravenshaw College. It is the tradition in this department that students from your college always top. Promise that you won't let me down." That was the level of encouragement at IIT. Teachers like Professor P K Bhattacharya, ever-smiling and handsome, popularly known to students and colleagues as PKB who excelled in teaching, and at music, Russian ballet (PKB had presented ballet on Moscow TV) and games; Professors B R Seth; S N Sarkar; S V L N Rao; Sisir Sen; Ashok Mukherjee; Khitin Naha; Dev Kumar Ganguli; Dillip Sengupta; H N Bose and B G Chatterjee, to name a few from a galaxy of living deities at Kharagpur who lifted the students to unparalleled levels of achievement in science, engineering and humanism.

I had a special status as a leading institute volleyball player. I was nicknamed 'Olympian' and was later awarded the 'Institute Blue'. Being good at studies gave a personal satisfaction, whereas being good at sports gave a different visibility in the campus – "There goes the Olympian" gave a great feeling, indeed. IIT fills the students with new knowledge, new confidence, new enthusiasm, self-respect (often misinterpreted by many as pride or arrogance; nothing of that sort though), an embedded work-fun culture and positive thinking.

After graduation I joined the National Geophysical Research Institute (NGRI), Hyderabad in May 1965 and carried out research under the guidance of a man who stood out for his hard work, knowledge, integrity, honesty, achievements and fame. He was Dr Amalendu Roy. Vishnu Sir had initiated my education with three perfect circles and Dr Amalendu Roy initiated my research career at NGRI. Roy Sir's association was invigorating and he remarked again and again to me "How shall I ignite the dormant volcano in you? "Roy Sir led me to take up challenge after challenge, and taught me not to be a mere follower but to be the one to create followers.

Together we could develop new concepts that were accepted the world over in different fields of geophysics — groundwater exploration, electromagnetic methods and potential fields. To me, Roy Sir is a great teacher who not only dominated geophysical research in India well over a quarter century, but also gave new directions in geophysical education. He remained honest to the core as a scientist and human being. He never took undue authorship of any paper.

Authorship-grabbing is a national as well as international issue that has marred scientific scholarship to a great extent.

Roy was clearly above this unfortunate malady. In the very beginning he declared, "My job requirement is to guide and conduct research: I am paid by the government to guide, so no authorship; I shall author a paper only when I conduct my own research." Such noble thoughts have inspired not only me, but many of my colleagues. The recognition of my research work climaxed with the award of the coveted Shanti Swaroop Bhatnagar Prize in 1986.

Lady Pacific
Devika Bose

It was the summer of 1977. I was critically ill with a disease which prevented me from going out, or studying. I had taken my BA (Honours) Examination. The Jadavpur University had already advertised admissions to its MA program. My doctor advised my parents to get me admitted to ensure a speedy recovery. But the future was bleak in front of us because there was no one to stand by our side to guide me through the admission tests and other related procedures. It was then that I approached Professor Sengupta, my teacher at Presidency College, Kolkata.

Professor Kajal Sengupta is a legendary name in the academic circles of West Bengal. A graduate from Oxford (1955-58), she joined Presidency College, Kolkata in 1959 as the first lady lecturer in West Bengal Education Service. Short and petite, extremely beautiful and active, erudite and jovial, Kajal Sengupta was never afraid to face a difficult situation. True to her mettle she stood by me on that cruel day of April 1977 and changed my life.

Teachers, like leaders, are born. Teachers like Kajal Sengupta form a rare breed. Their lives are totally dedicated to the welfare of the students. When I asked her how she had felt as the lone woman member of the English department, she winked at me:

"Yes, those days were rather different. I was advised by my senior colleague and professor, Dr Subodh Sengupta, not to be too familiar with my young male colleagues, and not to dress up too much." We never saw Kajaldi in anything but white. Plainly clad in a simple sari, with her thick hair tied in a knot, we often saw her rushing from the library to the classroom or rapt in discussion with her tutorial students.

What was special about her was her total involvement with the students. In my tutorial classes she not only checked my answers, but she provoked me to question her from any and every angle. Just as she exposed herself to me, similarly she also had that rare eye which sees through the outer façade of her student's capability. Once she asked me to write about the love theme in Shakespeare's *As You Like It*. A few days later, almost in an afterthought she added, "Can you name the pairs of lovers in that play?" I, being the sly type, always skipping my assignments, had not yet finished reading *As You Like It*. I mumbled: "Rosalind and Orlando, Celia and Oliver, Touchstone and Jacques ..." "What! Touchstone and Jacques!! Do you mean to say that Shakespeare is dealing with homosexual love in *As You Like it?*" Thunder and lightening seemed to sweep me. Two seconds. Then she was off to the library. Collecting books for me, she advised me to go through the play first. Never again did I dare to pretend before her. The barrier between us broke down forever. I knew her, the teacher *par excellence*, the gentle guide, and the accurate assessor. She knew me, and made my years in Presidency College a time to remember forever.

Kajal Sengupta not only devoted herself totally to her student's welfare, but she was also quite open about her own indebtedness to her teachers. The way she spoke of her senior colleague, Professor Subodh Sengupta, and Professor Tarak Sen, the great Shakespearean scholar, conveyed her high regard and respect for them. She was a student and teacher in one. While teaching at Presidency College, Kolkata, she took lessons from Professor Tarak Sen, and told me, how after 6.00 pm a few teachers gathered around him to study Aristotle. "What I did was only to percolate a small amount of what I learnt from them. The nuances of each word, the turn and twist of each phrase came alive through their discussion."

Sengupta knew how to mould her students. Though there were no refresher courses during her time, she kept updating herself with the latest techniques. If, for example, I faltered at scanning a poem she would read with me the whole stanza, pronouncing and stressing each word and showing me how to mark the stresses. If I was wary about Milton, she would give me just the question I dreaded, to bring out the best in me. She transformed us, inside out.

Kajaldi was never actively involved in politics during the turbulent years of the pre and post Naxalite movement (1967-1972) while in Presidency College. But when it came to maintaining the discipline of the college, she was uncompromising. Once when she saw a gang of students of a particular political party mercilessly beating up another student near the grand staircase (leading to the statue of Sri Aurobindo), she instinctively stood in their midst and dragged away the boy who was taking the lead. The five rowdies then circled her and charged her. She stuck to her point – "If I see indiscipline within the college premises I would again react in the same way, irrespective of my political affiliation." Gone perhaps are those days of courage. Death is more proud these days and we are cowards!

Kajaldi was many faceted. When we passed out from our college she jokingly asked us: "What, studied in Presidency College for three years and not made any love match? That's interesting!"

Born on September 4, 1931 Professor Sengupta is now 72 years old. "I am not what I was," was her reaction when I contacted her before writing this short biography. But when I entered her house, I saw the same person, a bit frail, no doubt, but undoubtedly the same person. Her brilliant eyes softly perused me. She bathed me with love. And I remembered the lines from Keats's "On First Looking into Chapman's Homer":

> "Then felt I like ... stout Cortez when with eagle eyes
> He stared at the Pacific ...
> Silent, upon a peak in Darien."

Kajaldi was small in stature but when I stood at that peak in Darien, I saw a Pacific!

That Touch of Brightness
Kudlu Chithprabha

After attending class after class for 17 years, I feel sad to say that very few teachers remain in my memory. So much so that I had been conditioned throughout school and college to believe that teachers are not the way to knowledge. Attending lectures was only to meet the attendance criterion. I remember getting into trouble with my teachers for writing in the college magazine that the minimum attendance rule should be revoked.

When I left home a thousand miles behind for a university education, I had hopes of finding something different. Yet class after class passed by with nothing inspiring coming out of them. A summary of textbook lessons was all that we were getting. I was just about to conclude that the library was the only way to educate myself, when *this class* happened.

I still remember that first day and first hour. As usual I was looking towards the dais with a conditioned lack of expectation. For once, I was gladly mistaken. I don't remember the exact content of the lecture, my auditory memory having grown terribly poor due to years of disuse. But I still remember how that day, the otherwise dull morning entrapped within the four walls of the classroom had suddenly begun to change. The insipid air began crackling with mystery, with the magic wand of the teacher – Dr Suresh Kanekar. This may sound dramatic and exaggerated. But believe me, that was exactly how I felt.

As I sat upright, all ears, I was transported to a different world. This was not the world of textbooks that I had passed through year after year. This was a real world filled with real people. Freud and Skinner were no more names, but persons alive and kicking. Their theories were embedded in their lives, which in turn were grounded in the social realities. It made hardly any sense to study them out of context. The subject had a rich and interesting history. The study of Psychology didn't happen inside a drab laboratory in far away West. Just as it was connected to the metaphysics of philosophy, it was also connected to the mechanistic science of Newton. From the great debates of philosophers to the paradigms of natural science, nothing was irrelevant, and nothing was ignorable. More than learning who said what, we were learning the why and how of it. We were ourselves becoming theorists, if not, at least critics, no more passive receptors of doled out pieces of textbook information.

Just like life, the lecture wandered around without disciplinary constraints. No more was there a subject with conventional boundaries. Once we touched Skinner, and once Russell, once Einstein, and once Freud. Whether the building we saw outside existed, or it was our perception, whether we had really lived all these years or we had come into the world five minutes ago with the memory of such a life – were fundamental problems to be tackled. Theories of psychology came much later. Nothing was anymore to be taken for granted. The very foundation of our knowledge and beliefs was being turned upside down. I remember feeling breathless with excitement. The beauty of discovering knowledge is best at its boundaries.

Maybe not for all. Many, unfortunately, get conditioned to believe that the most important thing on earth is the syllabus, that the most important aim of life is to answer exams, and therefore, the most important duty of the teacher is to lead you to it. There was this very studious girl who stuck by my side mistaking my attentiveness for studiousness. During one of Professor Kanekar's lectures she nudged me, "Hey, what is he teaching? It is nowhere here", she was desperately hunting through the prescribed list of topics. I changed my seat the very next day. Later he was to tell us that he had nothing to do with the syllabus. That must have produced fear in the majority of the six dozen hearts in the class, though it was music to my ears.

The class attendance did get affected though mine got influenced the other way round; I bunked almost all classes except his. The thrill of attending his class kept me alive through an otherwise drab program. In fact, I was so fascinated by his lectures that I forgot that I had come all the way from home to specialize in counseling. I opted to specialize in the branch which Kanekar was going to teach. At that moment, I didn't know why I was doing that, I didn't know what it would lead me to. I just had one thing in my mind – to get the maximum out of Kanekar's classes.

Yet Kanekar was respected and held in esteem by all, but I don't know whether he really got the appreciation and understanding he deserved. I don't consider that *his* fault. He overestimated the quality of knowledge we had attained by then. He overestimated our motivation. Logically, only those with special interest in the subject should be doing a postgraduation. But most of us had come either not knowing what else to do, or to get a degree for the sake of a job. You can't blame individuals; that's how the system had grown. Many had got so conditioned to being spoon-fed for the exams, that there wasn't the faintest suspicion that there was anything more to education than writing exams. It is not fair to expect a postgraduate teacher to begin with motivating the students.

The great Vivekanand had once asked, "You might have lost sleep over so many personal worries, have you ever lost sleep over your country?" I believe Kanekar was the great teacher he was because he had lost sleep over his subject. Had we been students who likewise lost sleep over the subject, not exams, we would have indeed deserved such a great teacher as him.

Literary Blessing

Shridhar B Gokhale

The teacher who taught me how to 'learn' and think independently was Professor S Nagarajan, the first professor and Head of the Department of English, University of Pune. I joined the university department in July 1969. For fresh graduates like me, he was already a 'name' known for strictness and sternness. In one of the first few classes he told us about the Jayakar Library in the University and asked us to visit it. After a week he asked each one of us whether we had been to the library. Most of us had not been there and he asked each one the reason. I said that it had been raining very hard. In his characteristic style he retorted that the Meteorological Department had forecast that it was going to rain for the next four months in Pune. Naturally soon after this I started making an extensive use of the library.

Most students' college 'career' makes them believe that being a good student means attending classes regularly, taking down notes and reproducing them in the examinations. But here was a teacher who impressed on our minds that studies, particularly of the English language and literature, meant an encounter and struggle with great books, an attempt to digest them and give an honest critical response.

Entering the rich and spacious Jayakar Library was like diving into an ocean for most of us and we were completely lost.

Professor Nagarajan announced in the class that he would be in the library for a specific hour on four days and he would help students in looking for the required books. How many teachers would perceive the need for helping students in such basic ways?

In the mouth of a sharp but loving teacher certain simple-looking sentences become memorable and I cannot forget them even thirty years later. Initially during the academic year we had classes from 10.00 am to 1.00 pm and my friends and I would return home by the 1.10 pm bus. The bus stop was close to Professor Nagarajan's house and he saw us a few times at the bus stop. Soon in class he was to ask all the 1.10 pm bus riders, "Do you love your mothers very much?" We were taken aback by this question and hesitated to answer it. But he explained to the class. "These three students love their mothers so much that they must rush to them as soon as the class is over. They cannot tolerate separation from their mothers even for a few more hours." The message was very clear- that we had to spend more time in the library. This remark brought about a change in my habits and on many days I took the last bus home from the university at 10.00 pm.

Each oblique remark of Professor Nagarajan's was full of great practical wisdom and that was the 'essence' of true education for most of us studying with him. We often read critics' views on literary texts and reproduced them in our own term papers and examinations. Most of us did not strive to be original in any way and we were 'our masters' voices. A girl in our class wrote a term paper on some aspect of Shakespeare's plays and she reproduced verbatim passages from F R Leavis, a well-known Shakespearean critic, without acknowledging the source. Professor Nagarajan's comment on the paper was "I would have given F R Leavis 8 out of 10 for this brilliant answer, but I give you 2 out of 10 for faithfully reproducing F R Leavis." This remark did not allow us to be the same after that.

Sometimes the façade of tyranny teaches students what nothing else might teach. My tutorial group had 11 students and in one of the classes none of us had read the book that Professor Nagarajan had asked us to read. The excuse that most of us gave was the usual one – 'text not available.' This class was held at 1.00 pm. When he heard our excuses, he discontinued the class and asked the peon to get 11 copies of the text from the library and 11 copies of the dictionary. He made us read the text and held our class at 5 pm the same day. Most teachers would find this to be the best excuse for not engaging the class. We never again dared to repeat the excuse nor to attend his tutorial without preparatory reading.

Most of our teachers used to mark our assignments 'safely' by awarding us marks between 4 and 7. From such teachers the worst possible answer would get 4 marks and the best could fetch 7. But Professor Nagarajan had the courage to give marks ranging between 0 and 9 even in a subject such as Literature. Getting 6 marks or above from Professor Nagarajan used to be a matter of pride for every student.

Professor Nagarajan was a 'visionary'. He was able to feel the 'pulse' of English studies long before others could. He took the revolutionary step of introducing a compulsory course in English Linguistics at the Postgraduate level. Even if his own field was Literature, he was able to appreciate the importance of Language studies. During his visit to Edinburgh, he himself studied a course in Stylistics so as to be abreast of the subject he had introduced at the department. The University of Pune became the first university in India to introduce a course in English Linguistics and the other universities followed suit later.

Professor Nagarajan used to say that a first class of the University of Pune must also be a first class of the University of Oxford or Cambridge. He obviously insisted on establishing and maintaining international standards in the Department of

English. Professor Nagarajan has been a formative influence on most of his students. Being his student has been one of the choicest blessings in my life. But for him, I would certainly have been a very 'different' student and teacher.

Potter among Pupils

Viney Kirpal

Imagine you are a bunch of twenty year olds, attending a lecture on Shakespeare in the English Department of Poona University. The year is 1969 and it's the beginning of the session for MA Part I students. I am one of them. We are listening spellbound to our teacher because he is reading, no rather, he is acting out Shakespeare's greatest tragedy, *King Lear*. He is pouring his heart into it as if it were his own story. He modulates his voice like a Shakespearean actor, interspersing the dramatic reading with hushed whispers and long silences till we are sitting on the edge of the chair in suspense. He emphasizes words and language to force our attention to the original meaning of each word until after a while, even though he has not explained the text, the class has the feeling "It has understood".

For the first time we feel we need no guide to Shakespeare to help us read or understand the play. After a while the teacher begins to ask questions – deep, searching questions – that set each one of us thinking about the issues, the language, the dramatic form, about life itself. His carefully constructed commentary is weaving a magic around us.

You may have guessed by now that the famous Professor S Nagarajan, Head of the English Department, is teaching us and we are his students hanging on every word of his as if, were he to stop, the magic he has woven would vanish from the class.

For the first time, we were with a teacher who was making us experience literature and not passing his time or dictating notes to us for an exam. For the first time, we mere students, are being treated as literary critics in our own right. The Socratean method of questions and answers, the careful teasing of our intellect, the drama are all designed to train us to read literary texts independently, something no other teacher in college or university had ever thought us fit for. It is unbelievable.

* * *

We were face to face with a scholarly teacher whose mastery over the subject was unquestionable. He quoted like an encyclopedia, he connected different centuries and writers as if they sat in the same room. He did not teach as if he were confined to a particular course. And all throughout he was extremely lucid.

Professor Nagarajan was a very learned teacher. Till today, I feel he is better read than all his students, though many of them have earned formidable reputations. Every evening, you were almost certain to find him reading in the Jayakar Library, shoulders hunched, eyes glued to a new book or journal. He had dedicated his life to learning (his wife once jokingly remarked that he was wedded to his department) and he wanted us, twenty year olds, to do likewise!

He was a hard taskmaster who expected us to read, read and read all our waking hours. If we failed, he had ingenious ways of bringing the lesson home to us (Shridhar Gokhale's essay describes some of them). He didn't care if he treated us like school children. It was more important for him that we were trained properly.

For the first time we realized how much we were expected to read as postgraduate students. There were tutorials for which we had to come prepared by reading fat tomes outside the syllabus. There were also the prescribed textbooks which had to be digested, critics to be understood, journals to be read. I recall spending each hour of the evening and every holiday in the library from 10.00 am, when the imposing library doors would open, until 5.00 pm when the shrill library buzzer went off to alert readers it was time to leave.

We were in awe of Professor Nagarajan and his achievements. It was one thing to be taught by him and another to realize that he was one of the finest Shakespearean critics and he held an international reputation. To chance upon his papers in the best journals was a matter of pride. His example inspired. I wanted to be a famous researcher like him. I remember thinking to myself, "I too will write and publish papers in the world's best journals like Professor Nagarajan." He gave us attitude. He gave us self-belief. Though very stern in appearance, he always lauded our efforts and encouraged us even in our weak moments with his unforgettable comment – "Capable of much better" written neatly in red ink in the margin of our answer scripts. Seeing that remark, one's dejection would melt away and get replaced by a resolve to give one's best the next time.

Our teacher conditioned us into becoming researchers. He used to say, he'd give us 50 per cent marks even if we wrote about the book in our own words and hadn't quoted a single critic. "You must learn to read the text first," he would impress upon us repeatedly. Observations like this first set us on the road to scholarship. He taught us to be questioning and honest in literary study. The first ever assignment I turned in, was returned with the words 'Cite reference' scribbled in red in every nook and corner of the answer script. "What does that mean, Professor Nagarajan?" I took a bold step to go to his office and ask. His voice softened as he patiently explained to me the sin of plagiarism. As the truth dawned on me, I realized that since no teacher had ever before checked us, we had probably earned our BA degrees merely stealing the words of famous Western scholars, whose books we routinely quoted from without acknowledgement. This was a humbling lesson which left a deep mark.

He shaped us like a potter. He whetted us carefully day after day. He taught us in many ways. One day during a visit to the library, he discovered that a student had cut out the pages of a research article from a library journal. He was livid with rage. The student was discovered and I'm sure punished, though his name was never disclosed to us. However Professor Nagarajan spoke of this episode in one of the class hours because he wanted to convey a lesson to all of us. He spoke with passion that cutting out pages from library books and journals was akin to murder and concluded with the strong injunction, "You should cut off your hands before you cut out pages from a library book or journal." Both the image and the words have lingered.

To say that we all admired Professor Nagarajan – and do so till this day – is an understatement. We put him on a pedestal. On his part, he made us feel human – not faceless roll numbers. He made us feel we were part of his extended family. We could meet him in his office or home at any time – no appointment was needed. He cared deeply for each student's welfare and more than being a great teacher, he was a generous and great human being. It was that which bonded us to him permanently.

He first taught us that students are friends and a teacher must not stand on false dignity with them. He always wrote personalized notices such as, "You have to turn in your term papers by the 16th of November" rather than the impersonal notices we were used to, "Students are informed that ..." Everything was a novel experience.

He could speak of his problems to a student as if he or she was his equal. Once a student went to his office to find him staring blankly at some sheet of paper. Suddenly, he looked up at her and ruefully remarked, "Failed again. I've failed in Marathi again. Oh!" Clearing the Marathi language exam was compulsory for the faculty and his being a Telegu didn't make it any easier for him to do so. But with determined effort, he did clear the paper the following year. We got to know of that also. Such was his simplicity that it brought him closer to us even more.

Professor Nagarajan may have had his favorites but he was known to be impartial in his treatment of all his students. This impartiality was specially visible when it came to grading our term papers and answer scripts. You could earn A+ if you wrote a good answer, and a zero if you didn't. We valued his evaluation very much because we knew he would have taken the pains to read every word. He always gave us the freedom to argue with him over his evaluation but we invariably returned convinced he had been fair. Over a period this inspired trust in a way we had rarely trusted many other teachers, lively stories about whose evaluation were always afloat.

I learnt from him that one must read every word that a student writes and be able to explain to them why we have given good marks or withheld them since it means so much to them then. He also taught me that a student doesn't mind being awarded poor marks provided you have been a good teacher yourself and have carefully judged your student's paper before putting your marks to it.

Professor Nagarajan was around 33 when he was awarded a full Professorship and entrusted with the task of setting up the first English Department of the prestigious Poona University. A daunting task even by current standards.

The young Harvard-returned professor, the first Indian to have earned his PhD in English from there, must have dreamt of turning Poona University's Department of English into a department worthy of Harvard. He set about his task with great earnestness. He introduced the latest courses, the tutorial system and other interactive teaching methods, the practice of keeping (in the department's library), Course files complete with reading lists from every teacher and a date-wise schedule for the entire semester.

He worked very hard to achieve his ideal though he was working against many odds – students who mostly came from a vernacular medium, and fellow teachers who were sometimes reluctant or incapable of walking his pace. Once, word spread like wild fire that he had fired a teacher for not teaching us properly.

I believe he did his best to create the high standards and intellectual climate of a leading American university and all of us are grateful to him for it. He would organize BBC play readings of literary texts, arrange visits to film shows of famous literary works, invite eminent scholars from India and abroad to speak to us a variety of subjects. The exposure broadened our minds immensely. He even invited the famous Maxine Bernstein to come down from Phaltan every Saturday and train us up in spoken American and British English. No teacher could have done more.

Once, Maxine's class fell on Ganesh Chaturti, a university holiday. Professor Nagarajan announced that the class would not be cancelled as Maxine would be traveling from Phaltan by bus for the class. At the end of the class at 5:00 pm, there was a surprise for us. Nag, as we all used to call him, had arranged to send us tea and sweetmeats prepared by his wife. We were thrilled and touched by the professor and his wife's thoughtful gesture. It was a lesson many of us tried to emulate when we became teachers.

Quite understandably, he was my natural choice for PhD supervisor. As his student over the five or six years that I wrote the thesis, I learnt the finer points of researching and writing. He encouraged me, prodded me, provoked me to read, think and write. He wanted very high standards from me and wouldn't accept a chapter until I had fulfilled his expectations. Yet, sometimes when I'd ask him for advice, he'd reply disarmingly "I'm afraid in this you'll have to educate me." I learnt from him that humility and learning go hand in hand, and that a PhD supervisor and his student should be like good friends between whom there can be disagreements but no misunderstandings.

His sharp, critical observations, his command over the English language, his meticulous guidance taught me a great many things which I have tried to remember as PhD guide. In later years I did become a researcher and people say that I made a mark. If that is true, I can say to the whole wide world that to a large measure, that was the potter's doing.

Some Reminiscences of My Teachers

S Nagarajan

In 1958 I went to Harvard for a year on a Smith-Mundt (Fulbright) scholarship. I wanted to research in Shakespeare. The Smith-Mundt Committee was not very sure that they could award a scholarship for the study of Shakespeare, but I argued with them that Shakespeare and the Bible were the common heritage of all Anglo-Saxon peoples and the American contribution to Shakespeare studies was both considerable and significant. The Committee reluctantly agreed, and I won the scholarship.

I had thought for a long time about the problem comedies while I was teaching English Composition to Junior Intermediate students in the Government college in Amravati. I was a very junior lecturer, and the teaching of the Shakespeare play to the BA classes was traditionally the privilege of the head of the department although he was not greatly interested. I read the problem comedies for the first time in Amravati in a Complete Works. They are not usually prescribed for the BA, and the college library bought only editions of plays prescribed for class teaching. Since Harvard heavily influenced my development as a teacher and contributed to my professional rise, a longer account of my Harvard teachers and my association with them would not be unjustified.

My Harvard teachers, need one say, were scholars with worldwide reputations: Walter Jackson Bate, Alfred Harbage, Douglas Bush, Harry Levin, Herschel Baker, David Perkins, I A Richards and Reuben Brower, to name only a few. There were, I think, no women or Black Americans on the permanent faculty of the English Department. (There might have been a few on the Visiting Faculty.)

Scholars, all my Harvard teachers were, but, alas, I cannot say that all of them were inspiring teachers. The emphasis was all on research. But teaching is a different art. Nobody can be a good teacher without being a good scholar, but one can be a good scholar without necessarily being a good teacher. (It was said that Douglas Bush, one of the most distinguished scholars of his time and a delectable stylist, lectured to his shirt-front.)

I must add, though, that some attempt was being made in my time to improve the status of teaching in the English Department. Scholars who had acquired a reputation for teaching were being brought in, Reuben Brower, for instance from Amherst College. My intention in these remarks is not to criticize the distinguished Harvard scholars who shared their learning with me, but to emphasize the importance of teaching which is being downgraded nowadays in making academic appointments. Students at Harvard in my time used to complain that they paid thousands of dollars and came to Harvard only to find themselves being taught not by the professors whose reputations had drawn them to Harvard, but by the research assistants of those professors. Students are not intruders or eavesdroppers in a university. As I have said earlier, their innocent, even ignorant, questions can sometimes lead a respectfully attentive and sensitive teacher to new avenues of thought. This is my personal experience, and I feel grateful to my students for it.

My account of the Harvard teachers who influenced me should begin with Professor Alfred B Harbage. I wrote my PhD dissertation on the Heroines of Shakespeare's Problem Comedies under his formal supervision. At first he tried to divert me to some other topic for the PhD. "A lot has been written on Shakespeare, even on the problem comedies," he warned me. I replied: "That is good news, Sir. With so much written on the comedies, as you say, I can't seriously go wrong. Besides, you are there to guide me." He smiled, and let me have my way. I was what was called a Special Student. I was not obliged to read for any degree, and the Department expected no formal obligation on my behalf.

I enrolled in a graduate seminar with Harbage on the Elizabethan Theatre. The enrolment was limited to twelve students. In admitting me, since I was a Special Student and my admission meant that a regular graduate student who might have needed the seminar to complete his schedule of mandatory seminars required of a graduate student had to be kept out, Professor Harbage was influenced by the fact that I was the only graduate student who had already published in the *Shakespeare Quarterly* of the Shakespeare Association of America.

Harbage was an eminent Shakespeare scholar of his day. Some of his books and articles are still cited. I saw more of him than many of my fellow-students did. He had a rather forbidding personality. He was a severe scholar not given to making concessions in his academic discussions, or what is more difficult to appreciate, in phrasing his criticism. He did not always take care to criticize in such a way that the criticism did not hurt the student who was being criticized.

A teacher's criticism of his or her student should strengthen the student's resolve to improve. It should not drive the student to despair, resentment, or "rebellion". When Harbage returned the written work of a student, he marked only what he did not agree with, but was silent on what he agreed with or approved of. Such concentration on a student's drawbacks, however necessary, for the student to know where s/he has gone wrong, tends to depress the student, especially if the teacher is a distinguished scholar whose praise or criticism carries great weight. It is a mistake that many teachers make. They think that severity of criticism is the essential hallmark of a concern for standards in scholarship.

I remained in Harbage's eye because I occasionally used to 'fill in the blanks' when he could not recall a name, a date or the title of a book. Sometimes I ventured to suggest a different or additional interpretation or explanation. (Harbage always thanked me with an amused smile when I made these minor contributions to the seminar discussions. "Thank you, Mr Nagara-JOHN." (He probably thought that "Nagara" was my Christian name, and I was a "John" of some kind!)

I have said that Harbage was a severe scholar. I well remember the dressing-down that he gave me when I began a sentence in a post-seminar meeting with a tentative phrase of loud thinking. "I wonder," I began innocently. Harbage stopped me immediately and took me to task for speculating. Nobody had spoken to me before in that severe tone, and I thought that my Harvard days had come to an end. Harbage was after all the Chairman of the Graduate Studies Committee (or something of that sort), and was reputed to be the most powerful man in the department. When Professor Harbage saw the glazed look and the pallor in my face, he reined himself in, realising that he had perhaps gone too far. "'To know' is a sacred verb in the English language," he said, as if in explanatory or expiatory mollification. "We need more facts before we can theorise," he added.

Harbage taught me to distinguish between knowledge and opinion, although admittedly it is not easy to draw the line between them precisely or clearly in every case. Harbage, and my Harvard teachers in general, taught me the importance of going to the primary sources and the indispensability of verifying one's statements before making them. "Is it so? Let me look it up." I have tried to pass the lesson on to my students, particularly with reference to the English dictionary.

What Professor Harbage overlooked was that I was not yet tuned in to Harvard. Having come very recently to the USA and to Harvard in particular, I was yet to learn the idiom of Harvard scholarship. There is a general moral, I think, to be drawn from my experience. Young people are prone 'to wonder'. Out of this capacity to wonder and seek answers, comes progress in what we know. Sometimes young minds do go wrong or wander in a blind alley. But the hits they register are worth more than the mistakes they may make in the process.

Harbage's mind was positivist, and positivism has its virtues and limitations. I am glad to say that Professor Harbage and I got to know each other better, and I realized that his severity of speech and manner was the result of his passion for verifiable knowledge. And it was a teaching method intended to teach intellectual discipline and the difference between primary evidence and deduction or inference.

To discuss what one got out of Harvard without adverting, however briefly, to the spirit of intense competition that obtains there and what it may do to a more or less ordinary personality would be to ignore an essential feature of Harvard life. This not the place to debate the pros and cons of competition in education, even if we are agreed on the larger, more complex question of what it means to educate a human being in knowledge and loving-kindness, but this much is certain that competition affects our attitude to life and the world in general, both the inner world of ourselves and the outer world. No doubt, competition helps to discover talent and gift, but it also tends to downplay the need for cooperation and it tends to make material prosperity the supreme criterion of success in life.

I remonstrated with Professor Harbage once on the severity of the competition, but he brushed my doubts aside (Those were the days of Yuri Gagarin.) "Standards must be kept up, America expects that they will be kept up here. If they are not kept up here, they will not be kept up anywhere else in America," he declared. A bit lofty, even parochial, but it showed a keen awareness of the responsibilities of being Harvard. Competition raises standards. That insistence on preserving standards is a lesson not yet learnt in India; elitism in education is not incompatible with democracy in politics although the mode of reconciling their legitimate claims at any given time may well vary.

The second Harvard teacher whom I write about now, Professor Herschel Baker, was the second reader of my PhD dissertation. He was a patient, kindly man who knew how to listen to his students with encouraging, even respectful attention. I have a special reason to remember Professor Baker with gratitude. I feel grateful to him not only for the intellectual debt that a student owes to his instructor (I read Reformation Literature with him) but also for his generous and timely support when my continuance at Harvard for a second year hung in the balance, or rather, was in peril.

Not all our debts to our teachers are purely intellectual. Sometimes the gratitude is for a word of sympathy or courage or appreciation, or for support at a critical moment in one's life. This is the kind of debt that I owe to Professor Baker, and I am very glad to put it on record now as Harvard retreats into a dimming memory. My Smith-Mundt scholarship was coming to an end at the end of the first year. Out of pique or ignorance or overconfidence, I had not applied to any other university for admission to the PhD program with full financial support. As I recall fifty years later there were only three PhD scholarships available in the Department which fully covered tuition and maintenance. Two had been committed to students who were half way through the PhD program. I was competing for the third scholarship with an applicant who, Harbage told me later, held degrees from Princeton and Oxford. My MA was an external degree from Nagpur University which, to put it inoffensively, was a less well-known university. (It is well-known now — for the wrong reasons.) I lost.

That was when Herschel Baker came to my rescue. I had written a term paper for him critically examining the thesis of the distinguished Spenserian and Miltonist, Professor A S P Wodehouse of Toronto, that the second book of Spenser's *The Faerie Queene* was established in the order of nature while the first book belonged to the order of grace. The thesis was an accepted classic of modern Spenser criticism. I analyzed the second book to argue that the thesis was unlikely. My paper made a stir in the Department. It was deposited in the Graduate Library for other graduate students of Renaissance Literature to read. Baker who was deeply impressed with my paper took the initiative to argue in the Committee that something must be done to enable me to stay on for a second year at Harvard and complete the PhD. A needy student who had shown promise must not be turned away from Harvard since it was Harvard's policy that no one who wished to and was qualified to study at Harvard should be prevented by lack of means from doing so. (I believe that this is still Harvard's policy.)

The Department held a three-way conference with the Federal Office in Washington (DC) which awarded the Smith-Mundt scholarships and the Institute of International Education in New York which administered the scheme and the Graduate School of Arts and Sciences and convincingly argued the case for the renewal of my scholarship. There was only one scholarship for renewal, and the competition was fierce. There were applicants whose studies were more obviously "useful" to

India. To prove how earnest they were, Harvard created a special fellowship for me that took care of my tuition, while the Smith-Mundt renewal paid my maintenance. The renewal came through in a day. I owe this renewal and the special fellowship to the initiative that Professor Baker took.

I had courses with Professors W J Bate, R A Brower and David Perkins. In all their courses I was graded 'A' and the professors concerned invited me to choose a PhD topic from their respective fields of study. But I had committed myself to the study of Shakespeare's problem comedies.

One other pleasant memory must be mentioned here because it shows the temper of the professors I had the good fortune to associate with and it calls into question the belief among many students that Harvard professors are distant and not easily approached. I had written a paper for David Perkins on the influence of the Bhagavad Gita on the intellectual framework of Matthew Arnold's dramatic poem, "Empedocles on Etna". I revised the paper in the light of Professor Perkins's comments and took it to Professor Howard Mumford Jones for comment. Professor Jones was an acknowledged authority on American and British Literature of the Victorian era. His secretary told me that he had gone to California to give a talk, but he was expected back on that day. She was very doubtful whether he would come in. He had no appointments for the day. It was a long flight from the West Coast – those were pre-jet days – and he would be naturally tired. As she was finishing, in walked Professor Jones himself. He asked the secretary what it was about since he had not fixed any engagements for the day. The secretary explained, and I said I would come on some other more convenient day. Professor Jones went into his room, and a moment later we heard his large voice asking the secretary to send me in. He waved me into a chair, and told me to read the paper. He listened to me intently, and after I had finished, suggested a few changes and asked me to send it for publication in the journal, *Comparative Literature*. (In due course it appeared there.)

Professor Jones had flown three thousand miles, all the way from California, and he had come straight from the airport to his office. He was tired, and he was not a young man. I had no appointment with him. But nothing of all this mattered. Here was a young man who had come with a paper that seemed to break new ground. He must not be put off or asked to come on another day. This experience weighed with me when, years later, at the Poona University, a girl walked into my room in the late evening as I was getting ready to go home. She had a complaint. Her paper had been graded wrongly, and it was obvious that the instructor of the course had not read it with care. I took the paper from her, and as I read it, I realized that the complaint was justified; the instructor had been somewhat casual. I had the paper reread and had the grade revised. I could have revised the grade myself since, as Head of the Department, I had the powers, but the moral would have been lost on the instructor and she might have felt hurt at being superseded.

I attended Professor Jones's lectures on American Literature with which I was only casually acquainted. Not only was Professor Jones an authority on American Literature whose lectures were an experience not to be missed, but I had begun to feel that we should introduce the study of American Literature in our colleges and universities. Professor Jones's lectures were beautifully structured and were models of analytical and expository lucidity. Before he began the lecture he would explain what he was going to do, and write the main points of the lecture on the board, and at the end he would give a gist of what he had said and he would invite questions. The method did not leave much scope for the unexpected idea, the inspired improvisation which makes the lecturer a living, dynamic presence in the class and keeps the students on their intellectual toes, as it were, but it made for the easy comprehension of the lecture and its retention in memory. I have followed the method on occasion.

Probably the best-known teacher at Harvard that I studied with was I A Richards. He had a formidable reputation. He was a university professor, ie, he was not attached to any particular department. A Harvard University Professor (Amartya Sen is a recent example) is a professor who is working on the frontiers of knowledge in several fields and is distinguished as an interdisciplinary scholar. Richards was deeply interested in several things: the integration of the sciences with the humanities, the application of modern technology to teaching, the teaching of elementary English, the problems of poetics and the theory of interpretation. It was said that his classes in Practical Criticism (in Cambridge, England) drew hundreds. The book of that name which was based on the lectures he had given in those classes had a world-wide influence.

But his experience of the classes had made him feel that some of the brightest young minds of his generation made gross mistakes in interpreting a passage of verse or prose. He traced their inability to do so to the way they had learnt or had been taught the language in the early stages of their language education. The conclusion was that attempts at improving means of comprehension and communication should begin in the schools. Having come to this conclusion it was logical and also daring on Richards's part to migrate from the university teaching of literature to research in the theory of interpretation and the teaching of elementary English.

With the help of a gifted language teacher, Miss Christene Gibson, he established an English Language Institute at Harvard, and produced a series of books entitled *English Through Pictures, French Through Pictures, German Through Pictures,* etc. The books aligned simple sentences with stick-figure illustrations to bring home the point that interpretation must take the context or situation of the utterance into account. The books were based on a strictly controlled and graded syntax and vocabulary which Richards adapted from the syntax and vocabulary of Basic English, the invention of his one-time friend, collaborator and linguistic genius, C K Ogden. ('Basic' stood for 'British, American, Scientific, International, Commercial'). The books also reflected Richards's larger concerns about the world, and he sought to introduce the learner to some of the concepts that the learner would encounter in living and learning. Since I was interested in poetics and in the teaching of English in India and believed that early learning should be based on the fundamentals of language and be concerned with conceptual fundamentals and since Richards's name was one to conjure with, I joined his institute.

I took some courses on the teaching of English with Miss Gibson, and with Richards himself I took a course on Poetics. Again the enrolment was very limited. What won me admission to his course was an essay that I wrote on how I had been taught English when I was young. (He was highly amused by it.) Richards's classroom teaching was unusual; he seemed to wander in a monologue-like manner which left the class puzzled – till the hour almost ended. And then suddenly he would bring all the threads together and tie them up to make a discourse. Many of my course-mates were puzzled and even exasperated, but to those of us who were looking for mental stimulus, the method was exhilarating.

What did I learn from Richards? I think he taught me to be open-minded, a lesson that, alas, I can only claim to have learnt indifferently. He was fond of quoting the distinguished astronomer Harlow Shapley's "What has been concluded that we should conclude anything about it?" Talking to Richards, I can remember, I felt that nothing mattered to him except the truth, and he would go where the argument led him. Not all will agree. They may think that this is a rather romantic view of Richards and that he had an axe to grind. "Welsh magic," said Professor L C Knights skeptically when I shared my view of Richards with him.

Harvard is more, much more, than libraries, laboratories and libraries. It is a temper of mind, an outlook, an ethos to be savored at leisure. You must live in Harvard for at least four or five years to experience Harvard and allow Harvard to shape your mind and sensibility and condition your reflexes. It is a mistake to dash into the Yard with a satchel of books and dash out clutching a gown, a mortar-board and a degree diploma. I am afraid I made that mistake. (I finished the PhD program in 23 months at the end of 1960.) I doubt if I could have easily avoided the mistake. I was in government service with limited leave of absence for my studies. I suffered from the usual malaise of loneliness and the cultural alienation of a visitor from a very different cultural matrix, a highly traditional society. An orthodox upbringing was also a burden to carry. Besides I was also in a hurry to get back and "serve the country", if I may use a foreign phrase from a foreign tongue. Things have changed. It is useless to regret the change. The generation that succeeds us will find its own ways of coping with the change. "Romantic Ireland's dead and gone, /It's with O'Leary in the grave." (I quote Yeats from a failing memory. I had typed 'falling' – which also makes sense!)

These then were some of my *vidyagurus* at Harvard. What did they, Harvard in general, teach me on the whole? They taught me to care for scholarship although I cannot claim that I have been a notable scholar. But I have been a conscientious teacher whose teaching has not ignored relevant scholarship. Harvard taught me, again a lesson learnt imperfectly, the critical spirit, the habit of questioning unmindful of names and reputations.

It is a valuable lesson needed in a strongly traditional society and culture. Harvard taught me the essential need for independent thought. It taught me that after one has read all the books and journals in the Widener Library, one can no longer postpone the task of sitting down to think for oneself and use one's disciplined imagination; it is especially so in the study of literature. (I think it was Walter Jackson Bate who used to say this.) Harbage once told me: "Harvard can give you almost everything; but it cannot give you an imagination. You must bring it with you." This was in reply to my lament that Indian libraries were ill-equipped for research in Shakespeare. "What did Coleridge have but a copy of the *Complete Works*? An imperfect copy, modern bibliographers would say, but it sufficed him to write some immortal criticism." Perhaps an exaggeration, but the exaggeration of a life-saving truth.

Harvard taught me what I have tried to practice all my life even outside the walls of academe – integrity of character and spirit. (Harvard's motto is VERITAS, an ideal to be inwardly transcribed and put into practice to the extent that one's powers permit.) To be worthy of Harvard has remained with me a constant criterion. I have always tried to remember that what I do in any situation anywhere affects my students for good or for evil; what I do or fail to do strengthens that ideal or weakens it for some student somewhere. The conviction has no doubt made me sound, even in this essay, somewhat priggish and pontificatory. But my Indian students are generous and forgiving, and even when they mock one's pretensions, the mockery is an overlay on their affection. Most students are still idealistic in spite of our politicians (whom a former Chief Election Commissioner has called, in rather violent language, an incurable cancer of the Indian body politic), and search among their many teachers for a model. The expectation imposes a heavy responsibility on the teacher. For one thing, it restricts the teacher's freedom of behavior. He (sometimes it is a woman) cannot run about as he pleases; he will do well, certainly be more honest, to quit the profession if he wants to do so. (I say 'he' for it is most often a man who is tempted to 'run about'.) Harvard taught me that the price, though it is painful for some to pay, is worth paying, for it creates the opportunity to bring into being a few better individuals in the generation that comes after us.

More I hesitate to claim for Harvard, for I believe that the *vidya* that confers 'freedom' is *para-vidya*, not the *vidya* that is usually taught in our universities. *Sa vidya ya vimuktaye* that is learning which liberates. (But what is liberation? The Marxist and the Vedantin will answer differently.) One must not forget that the doors of heaven, as Newman said, open to the soft prayers of the saint, not to the insistent tap of the gentleman's stick though it is good to be a gentleman.

On this note, I close this remembrance of things past with salutations to all my teachers. *Sri-gurubhyo-nmah.*

This is an abridged version of the original essay which is in three parts. The first part deals with the author's Indian teachers, the second part with his Harvard teachers and the third part provides a brief conclusion including some reflections. I have included parts two and three here for reasons of space. – Editor

Investment of a Lifetime

Sampat Singh

One's full formal education takes generally more than two decades. Therefore, during this period one has to work with a large number of teachers. A vast majority of them impart knowledge to cover the prescribed courses so that the students can get through the examinations. There are, however, rare exceptions wherein teachers help their students develop their mindsets: beliefs, values and outlooks, which have a lasting influence on their lives. In this piece I want to narrate a few stories and anecdotes about three of my teachers who have, shaped my outlook.

It was in the beginning of 1946 that I joined the University of Allahabad as an undergraduate student. One of the courses offered was Money and Banking, which was taught by Professor R C Chowdhury. In those days the nationalization of the Reserve Bank of India was a hot topic for debate. Professor Chowdhury was against nationalisation. I tried to argue with him in the class in its favor. The universities were then not so crowded and some of us as students used to go and meet our teachers also at their homes. I tried several times to argue with him on the subject even at his home but he always succeeded in putting an end to the discussion to show me that my way of thinking was flimsy. To make a final try, one Sunday morning, I went to his home and sat in the chair in front of him and said that I was not convinced that nationalisation would not benefit India. As usual he asked me to give reasons in support of my stand. Immediately I said: "Sir, today it will be the other way round. You give me the reasons why you are against the proposed nationalisation and I will counter your arguments." Suddenly he shouted at me and said: "Get up and get out." I obeyed and as I started moving away he called me back and said with a glint in his eye "Boy, you have caught my trick! No more debate on the subject!"

In class, he always looked at me in a way that encouraged me. Perhaps he had seen some talent and potential in me. Two years later, I joined his course on International Banking and Foreign Exchange. By now he was very ill and finding it difficult to lecture, therefore he began to bring his notes to the class. He asked me to dictate those notes. For a while, he found the going good until his notes were exhausted. So, he gave me a few books and guided me how to prepare notes and asked me to continue to dictate them to the class. After that, his health deteriorated further and he even stopped coming to the class. As he had wished it, I kept the show going till the end of the course. Then the college broke for vacation.

When I returned after the vacation I learnt that he was no more. I went to meet his wife who gave me a copy of Romain Rolland's *Life of Vivekanand* with his name written on it by him. He had desired that it should be handed over to me. Occasionally I continued to visit his wife and she would feed me like her own child, at times instructing me how to properly mash the rice and mix it with the curry and then eat it. Every time I left after a meal, she would tell me she was fulfilling one of the last wishes of her husband.

Another teacher with whom I came into close contact was Professor A N Agarwala, whom I met as a postgraduate student at the same university. One day when I was reading a notice put up on the Notice Board, he came from behind, put his hand on my shoulder and asked me if I could prepare a note on 'Cheap Money Policy' and give it to him. I readily agreed. The next day when I was walking out of his class he asked me: "Where is the note?" I told him that I was collecting some material from the library and the note would be ready in two days. He said: "Forget it young man, you can never achieve anything in life." As it happened, later as his younger colleague for about two decades, I was asked by him to do many more things and I always made it a point to finish the task at a speed that oftentimes, he claimed, was 'beyond his expectations'. He was always in a hurry and most other colleagues found it difficult to keep pace with him.

Still in my twenties I edited an anthology: *Economics of Underdevelopment*. I tried many publishers but none was willing to publish it. I went to Professor Agarwala and told him of my rejection slips. He said: "I can understand. Will you mind it if I add my name as senior editor? Then leave the problem of publishing the book to me." Since it suited me I immediately consented. It was published by Oxford University Press and for long proved to be a global success.

Soon after the publication of the book, I was to appear before the selection committee for my appointment as a permanent lecturer in the university. I showed a copy of the book to the selection committee. Immediately, Professor Agarwala who was also a member of the committee said: "This book is entirely his work. I lent my name only because he was not getting a publisher on his own." Something more important needs to be added. The same day in the afternoon Professor Agarwala was to appear before his selection committee for his appointment as professor, and, three members of the two selection committees were common!

In 1962 I enrolled for a one-year course on Financial Management and Control at the Graduate School of Business,

Stanford University. Professor Pearson Hunt was Visiting Faculty from Harvard Business School for a year. I had the opportunity of working with him very closely. Professor Hunt was often called stony-faced Hunt. One morning as I was leaving my apartment to go to the university to attend his class, Pearson Hunt rang me up and said that he was indisposed and therefore not in a position to teach. He added that he had planned to teach a case study and would I be able to discuss the case in class? Instinctively, I said, "Yes" but, as I thought over his request, I could not find any reason for this unusual request in which a student had been asked without prior notice to handle a case in the class in the absence of the teacher. After the class as I was going out for lunch, I met Professor Hunt on the way. I asked him "Are you all right now?" He uttered only one sentence: "Congratulations for the successful handling of the case", and walked away.

Net Gain

A A Mutalik-Desai

Mine has been an enviable lot as at every stage of my education from the Kannada Primary School in my hometown, Nandikurali in Belgaum district, to my postgraduate studies at Indiana University, USA, I have been blessed with highly dedicated teachers. I cannot express what I have gleaned from them inside and outside the classrooms. In this essay I wish to remember fondly a renowned scholar and critic, an eminent man of letters, a professor of Kannada language and literature, the principal of Willingdon College, Sangli, Dr Ranganath Shrinivas Mugali (1906-1993).

I did my SSC in 1951. I did not know which way to turn next. The arts stream, I was told, led one nowhere. Science (and Physics in particular) and I hadn't gotten along too nicely. My closest friend opted for commerce. So, one sheep jumped and ... by mid-June I found myself in the First Year Commerce class in the Brihan Maharashtra College of Commerce, Poona. Within a few weeks, except for a course and a half in English literature, I developed an unshakable dislike for the syllabus leading to the BCom degree. Elements of Commerce, Introduction to Salesmanship and Economics, Elementary Book-keeping (on the Principles of double entry), Commercial Geography and so on. Was I going to be submerged in such stuff for four years? I was lost even as my classmates were excited about the prospects of plum jobs in banking, insurance and accountancy. It was a time of crisis for me and I was scarcely sixteen years of age, a small town lad in a city, all alone, for the first time in my life.

At about the same time I found a small library run by the Karnataka Sangh. A deposit of two rupees and a monthly fee of one rupee and, the treasures of Kannada literature were all mine to relish. Which I did before someone could say "Profit and Loss Account", words I wished so dearly to forget! Bendre's poems, Karanth's novels and Rangacharya's plays were in my hands: "Then felt I like some watcher of the skies / When a new planet swims into his ken." My firmament was suddenly filled with numerous new planets. Around that time, I had also started reading in English (prompted undoubtedly by the inspiring lectures by Professors Murdeshwar and Bhagwat on Thomas Hardy, E M Forster, and the English one-act plays, short stories and essays). But at BMCC I remained a weary passerby; at the Karnataka Sangh I was an avid explorer.

In Poona there was a University of Poona Association of Kannada Students. Before the first term was over, I had listened to the talks and recitals of poetry by the poet laureate of modern Karnataka, D R Bendre, and Professor Mugali. While the former inspired me to dream dreams of poetry, the latter helped me in a most pragmatic and avuncular way, and it is this role he played in my life which is the subject of this essay. It is something that I wish to remember, record my gratitude, alas, only through such an impersonal and unreachable tribute, as he is no more.

Even before my first-year studies at BMCC had concluded, I had resolved to give up my commerce studies and go in for a BA and MA in Kannada, and become eventually a lecturer in that new found discipline, although I did not know how to make the transition, nor had I even an inkling of the practical difficulties involved. But having resolved, I confided in my close friends. Their response was an unequivocal chorus: "You are a fool", "You are pursuing the most impractical thoughts", "You are betraying the trust of your guardians by wishing to move away from BCom," "BAs are turning towards a BCom, and, here you are wanting to turn towards BA in Kannada when you are all set for a well-paying job", "As a language teacher, will you earn enough to eat?"... and so it went. Unable to figure it out, I decided to meet Professor Mugali. With his gentle manner and personal warmth, I felt, he was the one I should turn to. I was fortunate he *was* the right person.

So, on one of his visits to Poona during 1951-1952, I met him. I was nervous and apprehensive. I was such a neophyte, and he a man of eminence. I was not sure whatever I was going to speak to him. As I sat next to him, uneasy and struggling for words, he understood my state. Generously, he made it easy for me to open up. He began by asking me about my hometown, my family, my education and how I spent my time off from studies. Did I read any poems or novels? He surprised me by telling me that there was much in common between us! We both belonged to a milieu (this last word I did not know at all at the time!) which was a combination of the cultures of southern Maharashtra and northern Karnataka. The food we ate, the religious and social rituals we observed, even the way we spoke Kannada were alike. All this put me at ease. Still unsure, I began to talk.

The gist of what I conveyed was: I was not cut out for BCom. I wanted to study and cultivate Kannada literature and become a lecturer in it. Professor Mugali broke into an unrestrained laugh which unnerved me. I was sure there and then that my mission had failed. I was uneasy. He sensed my unease. The gist of his advice was: In his long teaching career many young students like me had approached him with similar tales of their determination to do literature and dedicate themselves to the noble profession of teaching. But, you see, he added, it is always the story of a sea at high tide. It ebbs, the dream fades, and the students rarely ever return.

Then to more practical matters. Wasn't I too young to decide such matters on my own? Wouldn't my guardians mind such a radical change from a lucrative career to, at best, an uncertain one? *He* should consult them, shouldn't he? (He told me of some parents who had accused him of luring their wards away from the rich mines of medicine and engineering!) So, cautiously (and wisely, as I found it later), he laid down a few basics. First continue and get a BCom, and then join the arts stream and go for B A and M A in four years. Net gain, he told me, my time would not have been altogether wasted at BMCC as I would have a degree to show. Also in the process, I would have more time to think things over, consult my family. Second, instead of Kannada, he advised me to opt for English literature. The result: I would not be confined to Karnataka for a career. It would not mean bypassing Kannada: as it was my mother tongue and as I had acquired by then more than reading skills, I could continue my pursuit of it. Keep reconsidering, again and again, he insisted.

But he was not through with me yet. If I made demands on him, he reciprocated: he gave me a list of poetry collections, plays and novels in Kannada which I must read and write summations (almost critical appreciations) within specified time. I liked it. I complied over the next four years by when I had BCom as well as BA Honours (in English). In those days under the rules of the University of Poona, a BCom could do a BA, but not a BA Honours. Professor Mugali (well assisted by Professors T M Joshi, N R Kulkarni and Armando Menezes) got the university rules amended—just for my sake!

Professor Mugali proved to be as exacting as he was ever willing to support me. After BCom in 1955, I moved on to Rajaram College, Kolhapur, for BA Honours in English and

Kannada. From there Sangli is a short distance and so I was able to visit him frequently. During these visits (I stayed at his place now and then), he checked if I had done my homework. He spoke to me at length on ancient and modern literature in Kannada. As I sat listening to him, I felt that nothing else in the world mattered: such was his scholarship and such were his ways of articulating. From ancient poets like Pampa and Ranna, medieval and late medieval mystic poets like Kumara Vyasa, Basava and Akka Mahadevi to modern poets like Bendre and Masti, playwrights Kailasam and Rangacharya, he knew everything thoroughly. His knowledge of English literature was commendable too: to underline an aesthetic impression or an interpretation, he freely quoted from Shakespeare, Milton, Wordsworth, Shelley, Keats and Browning. In a large lecture hall, in a small classroom or face-to-face, Professor Mugali's discourse was as clear as it was erudite, as simple as it was moving. Those meetings with him went a long way in preparing me for my teaching career. Ever thoughtful, ever conscious of his responsibility as an educator, ever a true friend to his students, he went about ever smilingly.

Later, after my MA from Karnatak University, and a stint of teaching at the Sir Parashurambhau College, Poona, I left for the USA, but we kept in touch. But, sadly, I never saw him again. He had looked after me in a manner no one else could have. Like a teacher in the best traditions of this land, he had guided me when that guidance was so precious to me. What I owe him is immeasurable. Today, as I reminisce, I acknowledge my rich debt to him.

When Saints Walk the Earth
P G Joshi

About twenty-eight years ago, I had just completed my BA in English from a semi-urban college and was keen to do my MA. Dr S Nagarajan was then the Head of the English Department of the University of Poona and was very well known. The teacher who was to influence me most during the next two years was Mr Sudhakar Marathe, a young faculty member in the department.

I think the major reason for this was the personal interaction Marathe had with students. There were several reasons why I needed the kind of personal interest which Marathe took in students. The major one was that I had had a traumatic childhood. My father was very violent by nature and the atmosphere in the family was quite insecure. Living in such conditions for several years had made me very vulnerable, almost crazy. But when I left home even the thin guise of security of the family tore off, and I found myself all alone in the open world, lost, confused, in dire need of mental and moral support. At the intellectual level a similar thing happened. In a semi-urban college I was a bright scholar, but when I met stalwarts like Dr Nagarajan and Mr Marathe I began to feel very inferior. This was also because my classmates here handled English with ease and competence.

I do not exactly recall when I met Marathe for the first time, but I do remember that I told him that I came from Dhule. I was given the impression that Marathe also belonged to Dhule, but this turned out to be wrong as he had worked there only for a year.

As Marathe was friendly and encouraging, I went to him one day and requested him to visit me with his family in my hostel. He agreed to come but regretted that his family would not be able to join him. A day before his visit on Sunday, we finalized all the details. At that time, I lived in a hostel managed by the Students Welfare Association in Pune. As agreed, I received him at the corner on Chatushrungi Road and we came to the hostel on his scooter. As he sat on my cot and smoked, he noticed a strip of tablets on the table. "Why do you take these tablets?" he asked me. "Sir, I cannot sleep unless I take one of these every night," I replied (I had developed insomnia because of mental stress). My reply disappointed him. He told me not to take even one pill again and assured me that I would be able to sleep without it. Somehow, I felt so reassured that I began to sleep without a tranquilizer. After this, we began to go for tea more often. By now he had realized that there was something wrong in my family and that I needed more care and affection.

Days passed. During the second year not just I but all the students and Marathe came even closer. Most of the boys had studied in Marathi medium schools and did not have enough mastery over English. Also, they came from poor, rural families. The girls were from English medium schools, handled English with much greater ease and belonged to middle class families. Consequently, many boys, not to speak of myself, kept themselves away from the activities in the department. To overcome this problem, Marathe devised a scheme in which the English medium girl would 'teach' the Marathi medium boy. Accordingly, one Jyoti Sidhwani, with whom I had hardly talked till then, became my teacher. This was probably the most informal teaching-learning situation. The teacher and the student would sit at any convenient place such as under a tree in the garden, on the stairs to the department or in a room. There was, of course, no formal syllabus, no restriction to the subjects to be discussed. This provided a lot of speech practice that the rural boys needed and ultimately enhanced their confidence. It improved their accent as well. There was no formal testing, the student was corrected on the spot.

That was not my age to grasp the full significance of such attempts, but I now realize that Marathe had carried out a very successful experiment. Apart from some academic enrichment, it bridged a mental barrier between two 'classes' and helped us overcome our feeling of inferiority. This experience taught me that the more informal the system of education, the better the results. Also, one learns better from the opposite sex. This happened, like in other cases, between me and Jyoti too. Through the informal interaction we became as close friends as was possible at the time.

That same year, Marathe left the university quarters and shifted to Dehu Road. Everyday he would travel by a local train. On his way back to Dehu Road Station I would accompany him. As we talked, he often corrected my mistakes. Communication, dialogue, closeness was what Marathe stood for.

I passed out in 1977 and became a teacher in a rural area. Marathe left for Canada to write his thesis on T S Eliot. Later he came back, joined Hyderabad University and continued to pursue his academic work. We wrote to each other, at first quite regularly, then occasionally. Marathe had inspired us to pursue academic excellence and so, in spite of the discouraging atmosphere in small places, I took the PGDTE (Post Graduate Diploma in the Teaching of English) from CIEFL, Hyderabad, and the MPhil and Ph.D, degrees and wrote a few book reviews and articles and finally a book.

When I look back I ask myself, "How did Marathe influence my life?" and the answer is that he changed me in some very significant ways. For the first time in life, I learnt that elders could be loving and affectionate guides. My experience until then was that the elders only bullied, tortured and made life hell for you. It was Marathe's concern, which made me give up my sleeping-pill habit. He also taught me that the teacher-student relationship could be informal without slipping into familiarity.

When I met Marathe and his wife, Mira, I found that she called him Sudhakar and addressed him as 'Tu', which indicates a relationship of equality in the Marathi language. I think the seeds of gender-equality, the value which I have upheld in my later life, were sown during this period. The Marathes stood in sharp contrast to my family, where women lived in perpetual fear of men. I also learnt that for a teacher a classroom lecture on a given text, is just an excuse and the teacher must use it to expose students to new ideas and values. This is all the more necessary in a rural area. I think even if I have not achieved anything significant in my life as a teacher in a rural college, I have always criticized the injustice of the caste system and patriarchy in my discussions with the students. If some of my students may have changed their attitude in these respects the credit goes to Marathe.

Coffee with Archie

Ingrid Arnesen

> *I say to my writing students ...*
> *prize your flaws,*
> *defects ... these are the materials*
> *on your ongoing ...*
>
> *A R Ammons*

In July 2003, friends of the poet A R Ammons, aka, Archie, gathered to celebrate the unveiling of a plaque in his memory, near his usual table in the new Temple of Zeus at Cornell University (in Ithaca), New York. Archie had continued his coffee conversations there in the last years of his life until his death at age 75 in January 2001. *The New York Times* obituary described him as "an award-winning poet who could turn any topic, even a heap of garbage, into poetry," alluding to his 1993 book length poem, *Garbage,* for which he was awarded a second national book award.

Many of us who attended this year's gathering, recalled the high-ceilinged basement coffee house which was the original Temple of Zeus. The dark walls had provided the backdrop for the full-size plaster casts of statues from the Temple of Zeus in Olympia. It was a fit setting for Archie's early morning conversations, and he had welcomed us there through the years and seasons, beaming at the periodic return of former students; greeting us with both wonder and recognition. For Archie could perceive the uniqueness in each of us, even as he succeeded in establishing a lasting sense of community among us. When he would consider our poems, he would never seek to change our course, but rather encourage us in our own found direction. He would invariably bring along a single volume or journal to share, a new publication of his poetry by Norton, or a review of his work by Harold Bloom, a volume of Emily Dickenson, and often, a poem in his pocket.

As we would sit on the black wooden chairs beneath the 18th century replicas of Apollo, flanked by centaurs with missing limbs, the entourage would form a triangle in the mind's eye; the pediment the Greeks called aetos, or eagle. Here we would bring our dilemmas, photographs and speculations. And afterwards for me, there was always a sense of wonder at the world, the summer dew breaking into heat as I walked to my office, uphill, light filtering through the tall maples outside the AD White House, or the glare of a January sun on ice and snow.

When discussing poetry, Archie would be vehement about his insistence on the poem having motion : "It's the verb not the object, not the cumbersome adjective, as in dance, its not the destination but the journey that counts ..."

Through the last decades of the century Archie was my mentor and friend; the confluence of these roles is intricate and not easy. He had a profound influence on my life, perhaps greater than he knew. Today when I tell my research assistants that they can make a lifelong impression on their students, I am thinking of Archie. One of my Chinese students quoted his own professor in China who said, "Teaching is the most important activity, because only your students can carry out your research when you are gone."

Knowing Archie changed my life. Not only am I still trying to write poetry, I have taken an MFA in Davis and have visited Sweden to translate contemporary women's poetry on a Fulbright. Archie's presence is inextricable from this place, from this plot, from this landscape, from Ithaca. It was one of the forces that drew me back in 1982 to teach at Cornell. It is part of what makes this place sacred, magical or secularly spectacular.

Even now it is impossible to believe that Archie isn't coming back, that there will never be his eloquence at the Temple of Zeus; the matching of wits, the laughter and talk of the universe, dentistry and back pain, our sharing of photographs and grapefruit, or seeing his latest publication or poem in his distinct typescript.

Today, the plaster casts are dispersed in the university offices in various buildings on the campus, one of my colleagues sits beside the sculpted head of Hermes, another by a seated Aphrodite. The galley space has been converted to a lecture hall. The new cafeteria which has retained its name and a picture of the Apollo statue, is a low ceilinged basement room with a different menu but with the same bad coffee and plastic-wrapped muffins. Here, only Archie's plaque stands as testament. The landscape of foothills and glacial beds is bereft of his radiance.

The Excavation of a True Mind

Sugandha Johar

It was a hot muggy summer afternoon in May 1979. I was bored stiff working for the State Bank of India as a junior accountant and was not very pleased to be asked to open an account after cash hours. When I turned around with a bit of reluctance, I looked into a pair of the kindest, gentlest eyes I had ever seen. Little did I know that the owner of these eyes was to change the entire course of my life.

I started desultorily filling out the forms, but my interest perked up when that gentleman – Dr M N Deshpande – told me that he had just retired as the Director General of the Archaeological Survey of India. Always interested in Indian history, I had recently bought a book on Indian art and architecture, parts of which I was unable to understand. I promptly pulled out the book and asked if he would agree to explain to me the hard bits.

When I look back today, I feel ashamed of myself for treating Dr Deshpande with such familiarity. I had no idea how important and senior a person the Director General of Archaeology is. Neither did I know how great a contribution Dr Deshpande had made to historical Indian archaeology. Luckily for me, he did not take any offence at my stupid request, and agreed to help me.

After that day for the next four years, I spent every single minute I could extract from my work and personal commitments picking his brain. For the first time in my life, I had found someone who had the patience to listen to all my wild ideas and conjectures and then discuss patiently the pros and cons of every idea — however silly they might be.

Every time I had a doubt, or did not understand anything, he would give me books from his personal library. It was a different matter that I always went back to him with more doubts and questions. Now that I know a little about archaeology I can imagine what sort of a torture I must have put him through. Amazingly, through all this exchange he never once lost his cool or talked down to me.

Deshpandeji had come to Bombay to head a project for documenting the cave temples of western India. Even in his late 60s, he was full of energy and always managed to beat us in any physical exertion through sheer grit. No cave was too difficult for him to climb to. No ravine too deep or too slippery to walk through. All this taught me the importance of doing things with a passion, and the satisfaction of doing your best and then some more.

The stones and sculptures of the Western Ghats literally spoke to Deshpandeji, and he taught me to listen to their language. He showed me how to see, appreciate, and experience our wonderful monuments. That way he transmitted the spirit of archaeology and magic to me.

After that, there was no question where my heart lay. I had found my calling. I made up my mind to take up archaeology as a profession. However, to do that I needed formal training, and Bombay University did not have a master's program in archaeology. Once again Deshpandeji came to my rescue and told me about the Benares Hindu University where women could appear for the exams without attending any college. Not only that, he also coached me enough for me to stand first in the university to everybody's (especially my own) surprise! Even my doctorate would not have been possible without Deshpandeji who introduced me to Dr Dhavalikar; the Director of Deccan College who kindly agreed to be my PhD guide.

I am indebted to Deshpandeji for all this, but even more I am indebted to him for believing in me from day one, when even I did not believe in my own self, and making me realize the importance of following my heart when seeking a vocation.

Perfect Music

Gayatri Moorthy

Having been asked to write about a teacher who played a great part in shaping me, I thought I would share with readers some experiences centering around my piano teacher, the late Mr Harold Joseph. Having been a classroom teacher of science for many years, I fully realize that having to deal exclusively with one student at a time, is different and more difficult than the usual classroom situation where one teacher attends to forty or more students. The former can be very tiring, exhausting ... especially when one is teaching music. Which is one reason, why I have never taught music!

Harold was uncompromising in his demand that each student must give his or her best. There was no question of going for a lesson without having practised, even when one was an adult. And yet, when I complained one day that a particular piece was too difficult, that I couldn't do it, his reply was, "There is no such word as 'can't' in the English dictionary".

He could be very patient and encouraging, devising ways to help each student find solutions to their own particular problems. Standard exercises were rarely the answer; rather exercises were created and designed specially to meet the needs of the individual student. Harold was willing to spend extra time with a student, without bothering about the clock or rushing on to the next student. Pieces to be learnt were carefully suggested, so that each student developed an extensive repertoire. This is something that all of us who had the good fortune to be taught by him have always been grateful for.

While helping us master new and complex material, he showed us how to pay meticulous attention to all the little details that were written in the score. Thereafter, he rarely imposed his own interpretation of the music on us. Rather he showed us different ways to play the same piece and left it to us to decide what we would like to do with the music. This developed in his students, a real sense of understanding and playing music.

However, lest one think that this was license to do just as one wanted, let me share this little anecdote. I had just started learning a new work by Beethoven, one of the greatest composers of Western classical music, when Harold told me that I had not got the rhythm of the opening bars correct. He told me that he would not let me get up, till it was just right. As I remember it, that particular lesson, was perhaps two or more hours of torture, as I had to play that phrase over and over again, till I got it just right.

Under his guidance, I learnt much about the theory of music, and though it was not my favorite subject, today I am grateful for his explanations and examples. They help me understand what I play more thoroughly.

The need to pay attention to detail permeates all my practice sessions ... sometimes to my disadvantage, for no piece of music is ever perfect. There is always something that could be done differently or better. At the same time, the immense satisfaction that one gets when occasionally – only very occasionally – a piece that one is playing goes just as it should, becomes its own reward.

I am often accused by colleagues, friends and family of being a perfectionist. True, this same attention to detail tends to spill over into my working life as a teacher-trainer. I can never go to a classroom session without having prepared my work thoroughly, without having made sure that all my materials are available in adequate quantities and arranged in the correct sequence. The end product of all this preparation is a satisfying experience for both the teachers and for me, which makes it all worthwhile.

About the Contributors

Amar Nath Maheshwari holds the MSc degree in Physics from the University of Delhi and PhD in Physics from the University of Chicago. He was the Vice-chancellor of Cochin University of Science and Technology, and Joint Director, NCERT. He was Chairperson, National Council of Teacher Education (NCTE) till 2003.

Amrik Singh was educated at Amritsar, Lahore and London. He has taught at Amritsar, Shimla, Delhi and Patiala where he was also Vice-chancellor of the University. He has published about a dozen books dealing with education and describes himself as "a student of educational policy".

Anant Mutalik-Desai, a former Smith-Mundt and Fulbright Fellow, he has retired from IIT, Bombay, as a Professor of English. He has earlier taught at Sir Parashurambhau College, Poona, and Indiana and Fairfield Universities (USA). He was President of the Indian Association for American Studies (1998). He now lives in Dharwad, Karnataka.

Anjali Gera Roy is Associate Professor in the Dept of Humanities and Social Sciences, IIT Kharagpur. She has authored *Three Great African Novelists* (New Delhi: Creative, 2002) and published several articles on post-colonial literatures and theory in India and abroad.

Arnavaz Damania (b. 1938) was educated in Sardar Dastur Girls School and Wadia College, Pune. As a student, she played hockey at school, university and state level. She was President, Indian Women's Hockey Federation 1989-94. She was Judge to the Barcelona Olympics in 1992, and again to the Sydney Olympics in 2000.

Ashok R Kelkar (b. 1929), was educated in Pune (MA English Literature, 1953) and abroad (PhD Linguistics, Cornell, 1956). He has taught at Agra University, Deccan College and Pune University, Pune. He retired as Professor in 1989. He was awarded the Padma Shri in 2002. He has published 12 books, 100 research and popular articles on Linguistics, Literature, public issues in English, Marathi and Hindi.

Chithprabha Kudlu took her Masters degree in Psychology from Bombay University and PhD from IIT Bombay. She is Faculty Member, Center of Education Studies, Indian Institute of Education, Pune. She is involved in research and teaching in the interdisciplinary areas of education.

Chitra Naik is Chairperson, Indian Institute of Education, Pune. She was member, Education, Welfare, Backward Classes, Women and Child Development, Planning Commission, Government of India (1991-1998). She was also member, State Planning Board, Government of Maharashtra (1988-1991) and Director of Education, Maharashtra State (1972-1976). She is the winner of the prestigious Jamnalal Bajaj Award 2002 and the first Jan Amos Comenius International Award.

Cyprian D'Souza is the CEO of Kanbay India and the Chief People Officer for Kanbay International. He has been instrumental in establishing Kanbay's India operations. Cyprian specialises in Organisational Transformation and high performance work cultures. He has given consultation to companies such as KPMG Peat Marwick, Dupont, Taj Group, etc.

Devika Bose took her MA and PhD degrees from Jadavpur University. She is Reader in English in West Bengal Educational Service, currently at Durgapur Government College, West Bengal. She has completed a UGC funded project on Women Refugees and Displacement and has published a number of research articles on Women, and Indian English writers.

Gayatri Chatterjee began her career as a schoolteacher. She now teaches film studies in India and abroad. Her first book *Awaara* received the President's Gold Medal in 1992. She wrote *Mother India* for the British Film Institute in 2002. Penguin has now brought both. She has several articles in national/ international journals and is a singer of Rabindrasangeet.

Gayatri Moorthy, is an educational consultant in Delhi. She is author of several school level textbooks. She learnt the piano for many years under the teacher she writes about in this article. She is an active member of the Delhi Music Society, and has helped to organize many of their concerts.

Geeta Sundar (Iyengar) passed her MBBS (1975) and MD from Jabalpur Medical College (1979). She is a leading consultant Physician with over 22 years of experience in hospitals in Delhi and Pune, where she lives now. Her books, *Health After Forty, Smile A While Doc* and *Constipation Can Be Cured* are very popular.

Ingrid Arnesen is Senior Lecturer in the English for Academic Purposes Program at Cornell University in Ithaca, New York, USA, where she has taught for 20 years. She is a poet and translator of Swedish and Norwegian poetry.

Kumarendra Mallick studied in Ravenshaw Collegiate School and Ravenshaw College, Cuttack. He took his Master's degree in exploration geophysics in 1964 from IIT Kharagpur. Mallick has worked as a scientist at National Geophysical Research Institute, Hyderabad, and IIT Bombay. He has published over 100 research papers and three books. In 1986 he was awarded the Shanti Swarup Bhatnagar Prize.

K S Venkatachalam is working as General Manager, Human Resources with Gujarat Guardian Limited, a group company of Guardian Industries Corp, USA. He is an occasional contributor of articles in leading newspapers and business magazines.

Lila Poonawalla is Chairperson, DeLaval Pvt Ltd, and Filarozil Exports Pvt Ltd, and former Chairperson Tetra Pak India Ltd., and the Alfa Laval group of companies. Ms Poonawalla is on the Academic Council of Pune University and Member, Scientific Advisory Committee to the Cabinet. She was awarded the Padmashree in 1989 and the Royal Order of the POLAR Star in 2003.

Nalini Swamidasan (b. 1930) studied at Ismail College, School of Economics and Sociology, Bombay University, and at Elphinstone College, Mumbai. She taught at Sophia College, Mumbai, and at the University for nine years. From 1962 to 1990, she taught Philosophy at IIT Bombay at the Department of Humanities and Social Sciences and was for a time it's Head.

Nandita Saikia is currently studying law. Born in 1983, she began her school education in Cheshire, England and later completed it in India. Nandita has worked as a journalist, author, editor, website coordinator and also as the Content Manager of the Indian National Youth Campaign for the UN's World Summit on the Information Society.

N S Cheema studied at St Vincent's High School and Fergusson College, Pune. He joined the Indian Army in 1947 and was commissioned into the Poona Horse Armed Corps. He retired as Lt General in 1985. He has seen operations in the Hyderabad police riots and in the 1965 and 1971 wars. He has commanded a Mountain Division and an Armour Division. He was Adjutant General at Army HO.

Padmaja Godbole was born, brought up, and educated in Wai, Pune. She went for specialization to Canada. In 1990, she set up Prism Foundation's Phoenix School for the education of children with learning disabilities. It is the first such institution in Maharashtra. In 2000, she set up Prasanna Autism Centre, the only exclusive center for autistic children in Pune.

Padmakar G Joshi studied in a village school, a small town college and at the University of Poona. His PhD is in English. Currently, he teaches at the K J Somaiya College, Kopargaon. He has presented and published research papers. He also has a book titled *Shashi Deshpande's Fiction* (2003) to his credit.

Partap Sharma studied in Bishop Cotton School, Shimla. He is a playwright, novelist *(Days of the Turban)*, the author of four books for children, film actor and director of documentary films. His plays, *A Touch of Brightness* and *Begum Sumroo*, have been staged in various countries. His voice is well known to cinema, radio and TV audiences as one of India's foremost commentators and narrators. He is India's first voice trainer.

P S Palande took his MA and PhD (Economics) from Poona University. An IAS Officer, he is ex-Municipal Commissioner, Pune, and Director, National Insurance Academy, Pune. His books on *Liberalization* and the *Insurance Industry* are well known. He is on the Board of many companies and has served as chairman on many state and national level bodies.

P C Shejwalkar is Director, Institute of Management Education and Dean, Faculty of Management, University of Pune. He has taught for 50 years, and published 25 books and 600 articles.

He has founded and led many management institutes in Pune. He is called the Father of Management Studies in Pune.

Rajendra K Saboo, Chairman of Kamla Dials and Devices Limited, Chandigarh, the second Indian to have held the post of Rotary International President (1991-92). He is on the Managing Committee of FICCI, and has been founder Chairman of CII (Northern region). He and his wife Usha serve as hands-on volunteers in Rotary Medicare projects in Africa every year.

Ratna Khemani is the internationally known Director of the Pune based Academy of Natural Health & Beauty & the Center for Personality Development She educates poor children from her earnings. Ratna Khemani is an acclaimed personality counselor, and visiting faculty at management institutes and corporates all over the country.

Rehana Ghadially is professor in the Department of Humanities and Social Sciences at the IIT, Mumbai. She took her BA from St Xavier's College in Mumbai and MS and PhD in General-Experimental Psychology from Auburn University (USA). She is the recipient of several research/teaching fellowships abroad and editor of the book *Women in Indian Society: A Reader* (1989).

R K Laxman was born and educated in Mysore. He has worked with *The Times of India,* Mumbai as staff cartoonist for over 50 years. Penguin has published several collections of Laxman's cartoons in *The Best of Laxman* and *Laugh with Laxman* series. He is the recipient of the Padma Bhushan, and the prestigious Ramon Magsaysay Award in 1984.

Roop Karnani is a Mechanical engineer who, after working for 10 years at TELCO, joined *Business India* as a correspondent in 1989 and rose to become its Principal Correspondent. He is

Director of *Inspirations,* an event management and public relations company set up by him. He has written a biography of the late H K Firodia.

Sampat Singh has studied at Allahabad, Stanford and Harvard Universities. He has taught at Allahabad University, the National Institute of Bank Management (NIBM), Pune, and IIM Ahmedabad. Professor Singh's publications include *Economics of Underdevelopment* (OUP, 1958) and *Leading: Lessons from Literature* (Sage, 2003).

Sharu S Rangnekar is a Chemical Engineer from Bombay and reveived an MBA degree from the USA. He researched in Mathematical Economics at the Carnegie-Mellon University, Pittsburgh, USA. He took early retirement from Searle (India) as its Managing Director in 1978. He has lectured and given consultations in India and abroad. His books are management classics.

S K Savanur completed his MSc in Applied Maths and PhD in Library & Information Science from Karnataka University. He did MLib was from Bombay University. He worked with British Council Library, Madras for 16 years and has been with WRIC Library, Mumbai University for 14 years. He teaches at Bombay University and IGNOU and is on many national level committees.

Shridhar Gokhale completed his MA (English) from Poona University, MLit from University of Strathclyde Glasgow and PhD from CIEFL, Hyderabad. He is currently Head of the Department of English, Poona University. He has written and edited 10 books. His specializations include Linguistics and Phonetics, English Language Teaching and Stylistics.

S Nagarajan was the first Indian to earn a PhD in English from Harvard University. He retired as Professor of English at

Hyderabad Central University. Earlier, he was at the Poona University for 16 years as Head of the Department of English. He has edited the signet edition of *Measure for Measure*. Presently, he is working on an edition of *King Lear* for Indian College Students.

Subroto Roy, postgraduate in journalism, is full-time Editor of *Education Times* and Joint Editor of a music book project funded by Sangeet Natak Akademi. A music critic and founder of Vazebua Sangeet Samoroha, Pune he is currently a PhD scholar in Indian classical music at the University of Pune.

Sugandha Johar is Managing Director, Productivity Council, Pune. She was educated in Pune and Australia. She is a well-sought-after management consultant.

Sushma Varma, Professor and Head of the Department of History in Poona University, was educated in the Convent of Jesus & Mary, and in Fergusson College, Pune. She took her Masters and PhD degrees from the University of Poona. Her specialization is Modern Indian History. She has published a book on Mount Stuart Elphinstone.

Vithal Vasudeo Athani holds BE (Elect. Engg.) degree from Pune University, ME (Power Engg.) degree from Indian Institute of Science, Bangalore, MS degree from University of Illinois, Urbana-Champaign, IL, USA. He taught at IIT Bombay from 1958-1970 and retired as senior Professor of Electrical Engineering. He has published over 100 articles and a book titled, *Stepper Motors* (1997, rpt 2002).